500 ELEPHANTS IN THE ROOM

500 ELEPHANTS IN THE ROOM

First Published January 2019

ISBN 978-1-9995850-1-3

Our appreciation and gratitude for Sarah Ray
who is
DESIGN MARQUE
Also her two enormous dogs
WHO NEVER LEFT
THE ROOM

Designed, Printed & Published by

www.designmarque.co.uk

Front cover image credit Moe Bura

DEDICATION

For my wife MOE love and thanks for the front cover which may never have been painted by her if she had not photographed the elephant in 1967 when she was travelling overland through Africa

OUR LOVE RESPECTS
EACH OTHERS STRENGTHS
AS WE BOTH SUPPORT
EACH OTHERS WEAKNESSES
WE TALK WE CONVERSE
WE MAKE LOVE AND LIGHT
OF ALL THINGS RELEVANT
ESPECIALLY OUR ELEPHANT

KEVIN BURA

BORN A GENETIC JEW IN KENT (1950)

CHOSE TO BECOME A

SOCIALIST

ATHEIST

VEGAN

MUSICIAN

POET

A LOT OF WORDS I HAVE PUT TO RHYME

ALLOWING ME TO BE OPINIONATED SARCASTIC

JUDGMENTAL AND AMUSING

SO FEEL FREE TO ADD YOUR OWN PUNCTUATION

BECAUSE MINE ARE IN MY HEAD

FOREWORD

500 ELEPHANTS IN THE ROOM is the 2nd book from KEV, the rhyming reporter.

In 2001 Kev documented Sky news every day for a year. Because of his disciplined daily routines and natural ability to use metres and rhymes, he was able to turn the news items into poetic unspent blogs. Joyful, or horrific news was treated with the same intense scrutiny.

His book, 2001 A WORD ODYSSEY is a poetic, historical, factual look into an extraordinary year that unfolded in front of his eyes. He wrote about BSE and CJD 'Killing fields of England' The 9/11 Horror, The Bush/Blair Iraq war and Terrorism.
The truth is still out there!

ELEPHANTS IN THE ROOM is an English - language metaphorical idiom for an obvious problem or risk that no one wants to discuss.

IVAN KRYLOV (1769 - 1844) The Russian poet often wrote fables that were rooted in historical events. He had a unique brand of wisdom and humour. He also wrote a fable entitled 'The inquisitive Man' which tells of a gentleman who goes to a museum and notices all sorts of tiny things but fails to notice an elephant.

KEV will stand up and read any one of his 500 poems which he composed randomly just as they appear in print. His audience can ask for any number between 1 and 500. His passionate delivery might make you laugh or cry, fearful, guilty or indignant but he speaks for us all and especially for the Elephant in the Room

1

ONE - THE FIRST ONE
THE ONE AND ONLY ONE
THE NUMBER ONE
I AM ONE YOU ARE ONE WE ARE ALL ONES
AND WE'RE ALL ONE TOGETHER
TOGETHER AS ONE
BUT FIRST
ACTIONS SPEAK LOUDER THAN PRAYERS
THEY ARE JUST SELF MANTRAS OF DISCIPLINES
FOCUSING ONES THOUGHTS AND ENERGIES
CONTROLLED BY ONESELF OR BY A RELIGION
SPEAKING TO ONESELF OVER AND OVER AGAIN
COULD BE CONSTRUED AS THE FIRST SIGNS OF DEMENTIA
THE THIN VEIL LINE ONE WALKS
CONSCIOUS OF THE PRESENT GIFT OF LIFE
AND THOSE BELIEVING IN AN AFTER
ONE MUST STAY STRONG
LIVE AN ACTION FULFILLED LIFE
IF ONLY IN WORDS

2

MAY WE ALL NOW FACE THE FACTS
IRON OUT ALL THE LITTLE CRACKS
AS WE DEAL WITH ALL THE CRAP
DEALT OUT EACH DAY BY THIS AND THAT
PLANET EARTH IS PLANT BASED
THERES MINERALS AND OILS FROM DINOSAURS WASTE
BEING MINED AT AN ALARMING RATE
POLLUTING AND SUFFOCATING THIS BEAUTIFUL SPACE

3

HUMANS ARE NOT BORN VEGETARIAN CARNIVORE NOR VEGAN
THEY ARE FED AND NOURISHED BY THEIR PARENTS
IN A COMMUNITY SUBJECT TO LOCAL NATURAL RESOURCES AND ENVIRONMENT
CHOICE OF FOOD IS A LUXURY IT REPRESENTS FREEDOM TO CHOOSE
HERE IN THE WESTERN FREE WORLD LUXURY OF FOOD IS ALL AROUND US
SO CHOOSE WISELY THE PLANT OR THE BEAST
IT IS THE SAME WITH RELIGIOUS INDOCTRINATIONS
IF ONE IS SURROUNDED BY CHURCHES
IF ONE IS SURROUNDED BY MOSQUES
IF ONE IS SURROUNDED BY SYNAGOGUES
ONES' SHACKLED BELIEFS LIMITS ONES CHOICE
AND ONES FREEDOM TO CHOOSE CLEARLY LET ALONE WISELY
FOR THOUSANDS OF YEARS THIS METHOD
THIS INDOCTRINATION HAS WORKED FOR THEIR RELIGIOUS STATES & COUNTRIES
WHY SHOULD THESE NON TAX PAYING INSTITUTIONS CHANGE
WHENEVER THEY OR ANYONE OF THEM
HAVE BEEN QUESTIONED INSULTED OR THREATENED
THEY GO TO WAR TO SAVE FACE AND KEEP POWER
THIS IS WHY I AM A SOCIALIST ATHEIST VEGAN NATURALLY
AN ENTHUSIAST ON ENVIRONMENTAL ENERGY

4

ITS CLEAR AS WE SEE THE NIGHTS SKY
THAT WE APPEAR AS A SPEC OF BRIGHT LIGHT AT NIGHT
A STAR MAYBE OR A DROPLET OF WATER
SUSPENDED IN SUPERNOVA ANIMATION AS ALL STARS ARE
AND ALL THAT SEEMS FIXED AND PERMANENTLY STABLE
LIKE THE SKYLINE ISN'T
EVERYTHING IS MOVING
LIGHT SOUND TIME AND ENERGY

5

HAVE YOU SEEN A MINK SKINNED ALIVE
THEY DON'T BLINK
BILLIONS OF RABBITS MONKEYS AND RATS
TURNED INTO COATS HANDBAGS AND HATS
BRED FOR RESEARCH AND MODIFIED IN LABS
ALL ORGANS BRAINS AND HEARTS
MONITORED AND TESTED
THE FEAR AND PAIN THRESHOLD OF
THIS TORTUROUS SYSTEM IS
USED IN ALL FORMS OF CARNIVORE EXISTENCE

6

WE NEED TO UP THE FERTILITY RATE OF PIGS EVERYWHERE
(the fast food giants of the west)
LETS USE THE FERTILITY HORMONE PMSG FOUND IN PREGNANT MARES

HORSE BLOOD FARMS
HERE IN EUROPE AND AMERICAS
HORSE TORTURE FOR THE PIG INDUSTRY
HORSE HORMONE PMSG PROMOTES PIG FERTILITY
10 LITRES OF BLOOD EXTRACTED AT ANY ONE TIME
DEBILITATINGLY PAINFUL AND NEAR DEATH
WHAT AN HORRIFIC AND MORONIC CRIME

7

COMMUNE PEOPLE LIVING TOGETHER COMMUNALLY
THEY COMMUNICATE AS A COMMUNITY
COMMUNITIES OF PEOPLE
COMMUNISTS MAYBE

LIBERAL GENEROUS AND TOLERANT
A GOOD ALL ROUND EDUCATION
FOR ALL PEOPLE
THE LIBERAL POINT OF VIEW

LABOUR SOCIETY AS A WHOLE
PEOPLE ARE SOCIABLE
THEIR SOCIABILITIES AND SOCIABLENESS
ARE TOTALLY ENTWINED WITH SOCIAL EVENTS
THE SOCIALITE MAY NOT HAVE THE SAME BELIEFS
AS THE SOCIALISTS SOCIALISM
THAT THE COUNTRIES WEALTH
ITS LAND MINES INDUSTRIES AND RAILWAYS etc
SHOULD BELONG TO THE PEOPLE AS A WHOLE
NOT TO PRIVATE ENTERPRISE OR OWNERSHIP

CONSERVATIVE DISLIKING CHANGE
MODERATE OPTIONS
MODERATE QUALITIES
MODERATE ABILITIES
MODERATE VIEWS
THE CONSERVATIVE
MAY ONLY BE
MODERATE
MODERATELY

8

COMPASSION IN FARMING
A R A B L E
NON COMPASSIONATE FARMING
P A S T O R A L

9

WHAT DID ONE DIC
SAY TO ANOTHER DIC
HI KIM
HI DON

10

AFTER SHARING
THE NIGHTS BOOZE
THE SELFISH DRUNKS
SHARE THEIR HANGOVERS TOO

11

WHERE DOES ALL THE RUBBER GO
FROM OUR TYRES
WHERE DOES ALL THE RUBBER GO
NOBODY KNOWS
WHERE DOES ALL THE RUBBER GO
LEFT ON ALL OUR ROADS
WHERE DOES ALL THE RUBBER GO
WE DON'T HAVE RUBBER ROADS
WHERE DOES ALL THE RUBBER GO
10% LEFT ON THE ROADS
WHERE DOES ALL THE OTHER RUBBER GO
UP OUR NOSE WE SUPPOSE

12

DREAMS LIES AND REALITY
ARE SOLD TO US EACH DAY
DREAMS DON'T EXIST
LIES DON'T MANIFEST
AND REALITY IS LEFT
BLURRED AND OPAQUE

13

SLAVE DEBTORS
WE HAVE BEEN FORCED TO BECOME
SLAVES TO OUR FINANCIAL MASTERS
THE BANKERS EACH AND EVERY ONE
MANIPULATED AND HOODWINKED
MANEUVERED AND EXPLOITED
WE ARE ALL THE UNDER SIGNERS
OF THE BANKERS GREED
THEIR FAILINGS CREATIVE ACCOUNTING
AND CORRUPT CORPORATE GAMBLING
HAVE COST THE MAN AND WOMAN ON THE STREET
THEIR FUCKING BET
WE ARE ALL NOW
SLAVES TO DEBT

14

HOW CAN ONE NOT BE
SOCIALLY MINDED
WE ALL LIVE
IN A SOCIETY
SOCIAL MANNERS
AND ETIQUETTES DISPLAYED
SHOULD BE BY EACH
AND EVERYONE OF US EACH DAY
SOCIAL BLINDNESS
TAKES CONTROL
WHEN THE POOREST VOTE TORIES
BELIEVING THE SOUND BITES
IT MAKES THEM A BETTER CLASS
WHAT
THAN THE HOMELESS

15

MINIMUM WAGE
MAXIMUM WAGE

16

HARD BREXIT

SOFT BREXIT

ENTER THE EURO BREXIT ELEPHANT

ARTICLE 50 IS NOT THERE TO EXPOSE

IT IS NOT THERE TO EXPEL IT IS NOT THERE TO LET GO

IT IS THERE FOR THE UNTHINKABLE THE UNIMAGINABLE FATE

THAT A MEMBER OF THE EUROPEAN UNION

WOULD EVER WANT TO ESCAPE

17

MOTHER EARTH SMARTS
EACH TIME A COW FARTS
HALF A BILLION COWS
BULLS HEIFERS AND CALVES
THE METHANE RELEASED
HAS HELPED CAUSED THE OZONE HOLE
ALONG WITH OTHER WASTES LIKE CO2 LEAD AND NITROGEN
JUST TAKE METHANE GAS AS A WHOLE
ALL OTHER POLLUTANTS
JUST ADD TO THE TOXIC MIX
MENTAL HEALTH ALZHEIMER'S
DEMENTIA DEPRESSION AND FATIGUE
THE GRASS IS ALWAYS GREENER OVER THERE
WHERE
LETS CHOP DOWN TREES
IT'S THE COWS CHEWING THE CUD
THATS AFFECTING EARTH YOU AND ME
STOP EATING COWS
STOP CHOPPING DOWN TREES
CHANGE YOUR DIET
BECOME VEGAN
AND HELP SAVE OUR BEAUTIFUL PLANET
FOR YOUR CHILDREN'S CHILDREN TO SEE
AND LET BE

18

EYE / EYE DICTATOR OF SYRIA
ALL OPPOSITION PARTIES ARE TERRORISTS
SO IF YOU OPPOSE HIM IN ANY WAY
YOU ARE BLOWN AWAY
ALL SAY EYE / EYE DICTATOR OF SYRIA

19

WE ARE BUT ONE
WITH ALL LIFE ON EARTH
THE STRUGGLE TO LIVE
MAY HAVE TAKEN MILLIONS OF YEARS
FOR A PLANT TO ESTABLISH ROOTS
IN THE RIGHT ATMOSPHERE
AND LIKE ALL LIFE
IT NEEDS TO GROW
IT NEEDS TO FLOWER
IT NEEDS TO SEED
METAPHORICALLY SPEAKING
ONLY THEN
THE MEANING OF LIFE MAYBE ACHIEVED

20

A QUAICH IS NOT A PLATE
BUT A TWO HANDLED SCOT BOWL MATE

21

CONSERVATIVE MAY
TAKES JEREMY CORBYNS SOCIALIST SOUND BITES
AND PERSUADES HER NAIVE AND BIGOTED FOLLOWS
THAT VOTING CONSERVATIVE
WILL MAKE THEM ALL
A BETTER CLASS CITIZEN
YET WE ARE SUBJECTS
WITH WIDE SPREAD ZERO-CONTRACTS
MINIMUM WAGE
A HANDFUL ON A LIVING WAGE
DISABLED PEOPLE PRESSURISED TO WORK
AND STILL OVER ONE AND A HALF MILLION
UNEMPLOYED
NO MONEY FOR EDUCATION
NO MONEY FOR CARE HOMES THE POOR ELDERLY
BUT WE SELL WAR PLANES HELICOPTERS
TANKS MISSILES AND TONS OF AMMUNITIONS ABROAD
FROM SAUDI ARABIA TO TURKEY
WHY SHOULD THE WORLD
BE RUN BY HAWKES
ALL JEREMY CORBYN WANTS FOR ALL IS
PEACE FROM THE DOVES

22

EVER SINCE THE INDUSTRIAL REVOLUTION
MAN HAS BATTLED WITH MACHINES FOR JOBS
NOW IN THE TWENTY FIRST CENTURY IT IS TIME
TO TAX THE OWNERS OF ROBOTS
THEY CAN WORK 24/7
WITH NO HOLIDAYS OR UNION MEN
SO NO TRADE OFFS OR TAX INCENTIVES
MAN DESERVES PAID TIME OFF TO BE INVENTIVE

23

AS ONE DRAWS ONES FIRST BREATH
ONE ACCEPTS THE PRESENT
THE GIFT OF LIFE
THE HUMAN LOTTERY OF LIFE
FERTILE MAYBE FOR ONLY
HOURS PER MONTH
AND HERE WE ARE
OVER POPULATION

24

WE'VE BEEN BRAIN WASHED
AND BRANDED FROM BIRTH
GIVEN A BAR CODE
AND SOCIAL NUMBER CODE
TAUGHT TO PRAY
AND TO EAT ANIMALS
WE ARE SCHOOLED IN KNOWLEDGE
THE GOVERNMENT SEES FIT
TO EDUCATE US
AND KEEP US SWEET
BUT KNOWLEDGE OPENS UP
A PANDORAS BOX OF WHYS
A GOD CREATOR SERIOUSLY
EVEN IF A SCIENTIST
THE SCIENTIST WOULD HAVE BEEN
A FRANKenSTEIN
NO FRANKinCENSE OR MYRRH
JUST EARTH QUAKES AND TSUNAMI
HURRICANES AND TORNADOES

LAND SLIDES AND MUD SLIDES
UNDERNEATH THOUSANDS LIE
AND THOUSANDS DIE
YET BILLIONS OF HUMANS ACROSS THE WORLD
ACCEPT IN LAW (for insurance purposes) THAT
IT'S AN ACT OF GOD WHY
IT'S NOT UNTIL ONE DAY ONE HEARS
THE WORD VEGETARIAN OR EVEN VEGAN
KNOWLEDGE IS POWER
POWER TO CHOOSE
CHOICE IS FREEDOM
AND THERE LIES TRUTH
AS RELIGIONS AND CORPORATIONS
GOVERNMENTS AND BANKS CONFIDE
WE THE MANY STAND TOGETHER
AGAINST THE CONSPIRATORS WHO HIDE

25

THEY ARE TALL WIRY AND THIN
LIKE THE HAIR ON THEIR HEAD AND THEIR CHIN
LESIONS AND GROWTHS GROW WITHIN
THEIR SKIN CRAWLS WITH PAIN
THEY LOOK ANEMIC
WITH ZOMBY LIKE GAZE
MOST WILL HAVE AN EARLY GRAVE
THEY ARE THE CHILDREN
BORN TO ALL
AFTER THEY CAME
IN SEARCH OF GAS NATURALLY
THESE ARE THE CHILDREN OF FRACKHAM

26

NANO BITES
OF FICTION OR REALITY
A TALE A THOUGHT
A STORY TO READ
TO THINK TO SHARE
SEND TO FRIEND

27

YOU GET THE PLOT
THE VERY LOT
IT'S ALL ABOUT
MANS OBSESSION
CRAVING TO EAT
THE MOST EXPENSIVE PROTEIN ON EARTH
THAT WALKS AROUND ON FOUR FEET
AND THE WELFARE OF ALL ANIMALS NOT
PHEW THE TURKEY SAID
MISSING THE POT
CHRISTMAS PRESENTS OF PUPPIES
PUPPIES ARE FOR LIFE!
A FEW ANIMALS DO LIVE A LIFE
BUT NOT THE MANY

28

MAY OH MAY
OH HOW YOU'VE GONE WRONG
SINGING THE TUNE FOR
THE FEW WHO HUMM A LONG
JEREMY JEREMY
THE CROWDS ALWAYS CHEER
YOU SPEAK THEY LISTEN
WE ALL WIN
THE HEARTS OF THE MANY

29

TRUMP VISITING THREE MAJOR RELIGIONS
ITALY SAUDI ARABIA AND ISRAEL
IS HE A DOVE FLYING WITH A WAR-CRY OR
A HAWK GLIDING ON A PILGRIMAGE

30

800 YEARS OF DECEIT AND LIES
NOW HEAR SOCIETIES SOCIAL CRY
FOR THE TORIES TO FEEL LIKE EXILES
LOOKING DOWN THE BARREL OF (THEIR OWN MAKING)
THE MAY GATE TRIALS AND TRIBULATIONS

31

INCLUSIVE CONNECTIVITY
WEALTH CREATION
INVESTING IN INFRASTRUCTURE
ROADS RAILWAYS AND BRIDGES
FINANCING RENEWABLES AND ENERGY PROJECTS
ELECTRIC AND HYDROGEN CAR CHARGE FACILITIES
BUSINESS FAST BROADBAND FOR ALL
TAX THE ROBOTS
MAKE LANDLORDS FIT FOR PURPOSE AND PAY TAX
KEEP YOUR MORALS AND PRINCIPLES
CLOSE TO YOUR HEART
AND REMEMBER TO LEAVE YOUR MIND OPEN
TO THE PRESENT FUTURES PAST

32

IF ONE FEELS AS BAD AS THIS
AS A PASSENGER WITHOUT COURSE TO REACT
PEERING OUT RED EYED BLUES
SQUINTING AND WIPING THE MIST OFF
TREBLED GLASSED HARDENED GLASS
TO FOCUS THROUGH POLLUTED SMOG
ON THE TORTUROUS RAPE REARING OF LIVESTOCK
CALVES WRENCHED FROM COWS
TO PRODUCE EXTRA MILK FOR LONGER
THEY'RE MILKERS OR MEATS

NEWLY BORN MALE CHICKS
THROWN IN BLENDERS
A NEW BREED OF CHICKS
KILLED AFTER 4 - 6 WEEKS
IF THEY STAND THEIR LEGS BREAK
UNDER THEIR OWN WEIGHT

THERES A BUTCHER ON EVERY CORNER
CHOPPING AND SLICING
THE RAPE REARED SLAUGHTER
PLASTIC WRAPPED TO ORDER
THIS BLOOD BATH
THIS TORTURE
IS SUBSIDISED TO THE HILT
VEGANS SHOULD NOT PAY
THE CARNIVORES GUILT
BEAUTIFUL SPECIES
LIVING PERSECUTED LIVES
THE FEAR THEY MUST FEEL
WHILST THEY SURVIVE
IF ONE FEELS AS BAD AS THIS

33

NO MAN HAS WALKED THIS PATH
WITH HIS HANDS HELD HIGH OR BY HIS SIDE
SOLELY WITH THE CONVICTION AND COMPASSION
COMPARING THE OH SO MANY POOR
PERSECUTED PEOPLE OF OUR SOCIETY
TO A FEW OF THE WEALTHIEST PERSECUTORS WHO RULE
AND HAVE MADE US ALL
SLAVES TO DEBT
FOR MANY YEARS DECADES IN FACT
THIS MAN HAS WALKED AMONGST US
HE IS ONE OF US
HE LISTENS TO US
HE KNOWS US ALL
HE SPEAKS FOR US ALL
WITH HOPE AND DIGNITY
WE CAN TURN IT AROUND
A SOCIAL SOCIETY
PROMOTING PEACE AND LOVE
HE STANDS AND DELIVERS
A LION TO A DOVE

34

WHEN ACCUSED OF BEING OUT SPOKEN
ONE SHOULD REPLY
ONES ALWAYS SPOKEN OUT

35

EVERYBODY LOVES ANIMALS
WHILST EATING HAMBURGERS
THINKING OF THEIR CAT AND DOG
WHILST EATING COW AND HOG

36

MAY THE BEADED LADY
WITH AN ABACUS AROUND HER NECK
OUGHT TO HAVE CALCULATED AND ANTICIPATED
THE BREXIT ELEPHANT
WITH ONE AND A HALF TRILLION POUND LOSS TO DATE
HER CONSERVATIVE DISMISSIVENESS OF OTHERS
MUST BE TO THE DETRIMENT OF ALL IN THE CABINET
HOW DOES THAT FIT WITH TALKS ON BREXIT

37

NORMALISATION
NORMALITY
NORMAL
NORM
WHAT IS THE NORM
SOMETHING THAT IS EXPECTED
LIKE A PREGNANCY
THE STANDARD TO JUDGE OTHERS BY
THE USUAL ORDINARY WAY
WITHOUT CHARACTERISTICS OR CIRCUMSTANCE
YET THE WORD NATURAL IS MISSING
AND NOTHING IS MORE NATURAL
THAN A WOMAN BREAST FEEDING HER CHILD
NATURALLY
THE NORMAL WAY A HOMOSAPIEN
FEEDS AND NURTURES
THEIR OFF SPRING
BREAST FEEDING IS PHYSICALLY
PSYCHOLOGICALLY AND MENTALLY
DEMANDING
FOR THOSE UNFORTUNATE WOMEN
AND FOR WHATEVER REASONS
THEY SIMPLE CANNOT BREAST-FEED
WET NURSES SHOULD BE REINTRODUCED
AS CALF HORMONE GROWTH FEED
IS KILLING OUR SPECIES

38

IF YOUR NOT BRITISH
YOUR NOT DANISH
YOUR CERTAINLY NOT IRISH
YOUR NOT KURDISH
NOR SCOTTISH OR SWEDISH
YOUR FINNISH
ON THE OTHER HAND
YOU COULD BE
ALBANIAN OR ARABIAN
AUSTRIAN OR AUSTRALIAN
STREWTH
A BLOODY ALIEN

39

DIPLOMACY AND DECEPTION
SMOKE SCREENS AND CONFRONTATION
BRIBES AND COMPENSATION
BONUSES AND CORPORATIONS
PRIVILEGES AND PRIVATISATION
WE'RE ALL SHACKLED TO OBLIGATIONS
AND AFTER THE LIES
COMES CHINESE WHISPERS OF
FAKE NEWS
TO CLOUD THE MURKY
WATERS OF WISDOM
WHILE WE ALL WAIT
PATIENTLY AND PEACEFULLY
THINKING WE'VE HAD ENOUGH
WE'RE NOW STANDING-UP
CONNECTIVELY WITH SOLIDARITY
TOGETHER WE SHALL WIN THROUGH
THE MANY NOT THE FEW

40

NO RELIGION HAS EVOLVED

AT THE SAME RATE AS HUMAN CIVILISATION

ARCHAIC BOOKS AND BELIEFS

HAVE STOPPED THEIR EVOLUTION

AND HAVE KEPT THEM BACK FROM SOCIETY

THROUGH HABITUAL ROUTINES & INDOCTRINATIONS

41

LET THEM PLAY ON PHONES

LET THEM PAY ON PHONES

LET THEM SPEND SPEND SPEND

ALL DAY ON THEIR PHONES

LET THEM £££

42

TONY CHARLES MIRANDA LINTON BLAIR
ON SUNDAY BLOODY MOANING
HAVING TO RETRACT AND APOLOGISE
FOR ANTI CORBYN RHETORIC
STILL STATING FROM HIS
CENTRALISTS VIEWS THAT
EXTREME POLITICS OF
THE FAR LEFT
HE CANNOT SEE WORKING
YET THE FAR RIGHT
CONSERVATIVES UKIP PLAID CYMRU
SCOTTISH NATIONALISTS
AND THE NOTORIOUS DUP
SO IT IS FAR TO GO RIGHT
BUT NOT FAR TO GO LEFT

43

YOU CANNOT COMPARE A COW
FROM THE AMERICAS OR EUROPE
TO A COW IN SOUTHERN INDIA
WHERE THE COW IS SACRED
YOU CANNOT COMPARE THEIR SKIN
THEIR HEALTH NOR WHATS WITHIN
WHEN YOU LOOK INTO THEIR EYES
WHICH ONE FREELY SMILES
NOT THE ONE
RAPE REARED TO BE EATEN

44

ONE HAS TO HASSLE FOR EVERYTHING IN LIFE

AND PAY FOR IT

45

IT IS ACCEPTED THAT RELIGIOUS BELIEVERS
ENCOURAGE OTHERS TO THEIR FAITH
ON THE OTHER HAND
ATHEISTS ARE NOT ALLOWED TO
UTTER ATHEISM
IN CASE ONE IS COMPARED
TO AN EVANGELISTIC
BIBLE PUNCHING PREACHER
SEARCHING FOR THE LOST
SOULS AND SINNERS
RELIGIONS ARE WALLS
TO PROTECT THEIR BELIEFS
WITHOUT QUESTION
WITHOUT PROOF
BEHIND THE WALLS OF
SILENCE

46

DAVID ATTENBOROUGH'S
DEEP BLUE
SEA
THEY
ALL EAT
ALL SHIT
ALL MATE
ALL FUCK
GIVE BIRTH
KILL AND FIGHT
TO THE DEATH
SO NO DIFFERENCE UP HERE
THAN DOWN IN THE DEPTHS
EARTH IS BEAUTIFUL
THE INHABITANTS

47

SINCE WHEN HAVE THE POLICE
BEEN A POLITICAL PARTY
PUNCHING PEACEFUL PROTESTERS
PARTICIPATING IN PROTESTING
AGAINST THE POISONING OF PASTURE LANDS
BY TOXIC CHEMICALS
AND AN OBSCENE AMOUNT OF
FRESH WATER
WHICH IS TURNED INTO
TOXIC WASTE
WHERE IS THERE
A SAFE PLACE
FOR ALL THIS
TOXIC WASTE

48

BILLIONAIRE BRUTES
BIGOTS WITH BALLS
BAROMETERS OF BUSINESS
BANKS AND BUREAUCRACY
BE AWARE AND EMBRACE
THE BOHEMIAN BOND
WHICH BINDS US ALL
THE MANY MILLIONS
NOT THE FUCKING FEW

49

THE WORLD IS FULL OF
FAKE BELIEVERS
IN A GOD CREATOR
OF SPIRITS FAIRIES AND GHOSTS
WE WERE ALL GIVEN
THE GIFT OF LIFE
THE PRESENT
TIME AND CONSCIOUSNESS
WITH FEELINGS AND LOVE
WHICH REGRETTABLE GETS
MIXED UP COMPARED
FALSELY USED AND
MISTAKEN FOR RELIGIOUS CALLINGS
APPEASEMENT AND ATONEMENTS
TO TEMPT ALL TO
BELIEVE THE UNIVERSE
AND ALL WE KNOW
WAS MADE BY A GOD
WHAT A UNIVERSAL PLOT

50

WHEN IS A TERRORIST
NOT A TERRORIST
WHEN YOUR THE OCCUPYING
ENGLISH GOVERNMENT IN NORTHERN IRELAND

51

WHEN ONES MOTHER IS SLANDERED AND ABUSED
FOR DECLINING A WEDDING INVITATION
AND A HOG ROASTING WAS TO BE CONSUMED
ONE WOULD INSTANTLY AND UNCONDITIONALLY
DEFEND AND REFUTE BUT NOT SO THE SON
WHO WAS BEST MAN TO THE GROOM
THE HOG IS REPLACED BY THE MOTHER ON THE SPIT
THE GUTTER FILTH LANGUAGE SPEWED
AND STILL NOTHING SAID IN A WORLD OF
COMMUNICATIONS AND JUST A FEW CLICKS
FROM WHAT YOU WANT
MANNERS POLITENESS AND RESPECT GO A LONG WAY
FROM ONE BEING MEAN AND OBNOXIOUS
CHARACTER ASSASSINATORS ON SOCIAL MEDIA
OUGHT TO BE RIDICULED BY THEIR OWN PEERS

52

EVIDENTLY WE MUST ALL ADMIRE

THE MASTERLY MANIPULATION BY THE MEDIA

TO PERSUADE THE MAJORITY OF THE BRITISH PUBLIC

THAT THE MOST SOCIALLY MINDED CAMPAIGNER

AGAINST RACISM OF ANY KIND

OVER THE LAST FORTY YEARS JEREMY CORBYN

TO BE PRO RACIST & ANTI-SEMITIC

RIGHT WING FASCISM AT WORK

53

LETS FACE IT
THERE ARE NO ANIMAL RIGHTS
ONLY HUMAN RIGHTS
AND THEY ARE VERY SKETCHY
ON THE GROUND
LETS SAY WE SOUGHT
ANIMAL RIGHTS OUT
WE ARE STILL BACK
AS TO WHOM SAID
WE SHALL ALL EAT THESE ANIMALS
AND NOT THOSE
THESE SPECIES SHALL BE RAPE REARED
ALL OFF SPRING WRENCHED AWAY
AT BIRTH AND SOUGHT OUT AS TO
A LIFE OF FEAR AND TORTURE
ALL OTHER SPECIES CAN LIVE FREELY
IN THE SO CALLED WILD
WHILST WE HACK AWAY AT THEIR
FORESTS AND SAVANNAS
WE ARE SOON TO BE
8 BILLION PEOPLES ON EARTH
HOW DO YOU THINK YOUR MEATS
GET ON YOUR PLATE
COWS ARE INHUMANELY BRED
A LIFE OF FEAR AND TORTURE
FED A RICH DIET OF BONE MEAL
(THEMSELVES)
LAST CENTURY GAVE THE SPECIES B.S.E
WHICH IN TURN GIVES HUMANS C.J.D
AND IS WHY NO COW
IS OVER 48 MONTHS OLD
FED SHIT LOADS OF ANTIBIOTICS
AND OTHER DRUGS
TO KEEP THE COWS HEALTHY
THE FEW WEALTHY
AND NONE THE WISER
STROKE YOUR LOVING HORSE
CAT OR DOG WHILST YOU EAT
COW CHICKEN SHEEP & HOG

54

SPECK SLAVERS
VISIONARY SURPRESSERS
TRIFOCAL LENSES
TRY FOCUSING LENSES
THE MORE YOU PAY
THE MORE YOU SEE

55

I LOVE MY SKIN
AND WHATS WITHIN
MY SKIN KEEPS ALL
THE BEST BITS IN
MY SKIN HYGIENE IS
HEALTHY AND CLEAN
LIKE WHAT I PUT IN
I AM VEGAN

56

A R T
DOESN'T GROW ON TREES

57

THE ANALOGY BY
DAVID ATTENBOROUGH
TAKEN OUT OF CONTEXT THAT
DNA IS THE BOOK OF LIFE
AND AS SO
A BOOK HAS TO BE WRITTEN
THUS
GOD MUST HAVE WRITTEN IT
BELIEVERS ARE STILL CONFINED
IN THEIR COMPARISONS BETWEEN
GOD AND HUMANS
THE THEORY OF GOD TO EXIST
GOD MUST HAVE BEEN A SCIENTIST
THE THEORY RESEARCH AND TEST
ENDED IN OR STARTED A
BANG

58

THERE IS NO DEATH
ON MY PLATE
NO ANIMAL HAS MET
ITS FINAL FATE
ALL RAPE REARED TO FEED
ALL THE DIETARY NEEDS
AND CRAVINGS OF
THE CARNIVORES GREED

59

DETACHED FROM REALITY
DETACHED FROM THE TRUTH
ATTACHED AND CONNECTED
IN ALL OUR STATUS FIELDS
BLIND REALITY
BLURRED AND FAKE
AS THE DREAM MACHINE WIELDS IN
ITS FABRICATED SHROUD IT MAKES
EACH FINGER POINTED
IN CONTROL OF THEIR CLICK
WHICH KEEPS EACH INDIVIDUAL
HOOKED
AND KEEPS THE CORPORATIONS
RICH

60

LIFE ON MARS
AMONGST THE STARS
AWAY FROM YOU
PLANET EARTH LOOKS BLUE
I SEE THE BLACK SEA
FROM UP HERE
DOWN THERE IT'S BLUE
SITTING NEXT TO YOU
I WANT TO SING
IT MUST BE SPRING
I'LL BE A DRUMMER
THROUGHOUT THE SUMMER
THE BAND IS AWESOME
IT MUST BE AUTUMN
COMPOSING SONGS
AS WE ALL ENTER
THE COLDEST MONTHS
BRING ON WINTER

61

WHERE WAS THE CREATOR
BEFORE CREATION
WE MAY FACE
ENDLESS REGRESSION
THE WORLD IS UNCREATED
AS TIME ITSELF IS
WITHOUT A BEGINNING
OR AN END
AND IS BASED UPON
THE PRINCIPLES

62

I'M MADE OF THE SAME STUFF
AS OAK TREES
I'M MADE OF THE SAME STUFF
AS APES
I'M MADE AS THE SAME STUFF
AS PLANTS AND ANIMALS
IN THIS PECULIAR SHAPE

63

IT'S SO EASY TO HATE AND DESTROY
IT'S SO EASY TO TEAR DOWN A DOOR
IT'S TOO EASY NOT TO CARE ANYMORE
IT'S TOO EASY TO DIE THATS FOR SURE
ONE CAN'T PRETEND
TO BE PURE
ONE CAN'T ACCEPT HATE
DO YOU CONCUR
IT'S HARD TO LOVE AND TO BUILD
IT'S HARD TO CREATE AND TO FULFILL
IT'S HARD TO MAKE AND CULTIVATE
A CIVILISATION OR A CALIPHATE
ONE MUST NEVER UNDERESTIMATE
THE POWER OF LOVE
THE POWER OF LIFE
WILL POWER WILL
EXTERMINATE HATE

64

I'VE BEEN GOOD
I'VE BEEN BAD
I'VE BEEN INDIFFERENT
I'VE SEEN ALL FACES OF MAN
I'VE LIVED WITH RICH MEN AND POOR MEN
BUT PREFER THE COMPANY OF WOMEN
I'VE TALKED TO BELIEVERS AND SCIENTISTS
I'VE WALKED WITH THE POWERFUL AND THE MEEK
I HAVE SEARCHED HIGH AND LOW FOR TRUE LOVE
FINDING YOU FINDING ME
IN LOVE AND PEACE

65

BLINKING THINKING
YAWNING WAKING
TURNING SITTING
STANDING WASHING
BRUSHING COMBING
DECIDING DRESSING
DRINKING EATING
CHARGING PHONING
SCROLLING MAILING
COMPUTING COMMUTING
PUSHING RUSHING
HURRYING TRAVELING
WORKING REPEATING
REPEATING REPEATING

66

FLOATING IN CONSCIOUSNESS
DRIFTING IN AND OUT OF
SLEEP WALKING MEMORIES
TIMELESS ENERGIES
VACUUM OF REMEMBRANCE
CORRIDOR WALLS
SURROUNDING OCEANS
OF POSSIBILITIES
ENVELOPING AND TEMPTING
COMPARATIVE JESTERS
UNPARALLELED THOUGHTS
EMERGING SOUND WAVES
ON A COLLISION COURSE

67

EYES BLIND OPEN
SEAS OPAQUE
CLOUDS SWIRL DARKNESS
MIST OVER TEARS
EYES SQUINT CLOSE
BRIGHTNESS NUMBS THE FOG
GREY DARK OCEANS
EYES MIST OVER
BLIND TEARS SOB

68

THE PETRO CHEMICAL CENTURY PEAKS
COAL GAS OIL PRODUCTION DECREASE
CLIMATE CHANGE REALITY
SET THE CLOCK
LITHIUM THORIUM AND HYDROGEN
NEW KIDS ON THE BLOCK

69

MAY WE THE PUBLIC NEVER FORGET
THE BITCH ON NUMBER 10 STEPS
WHO WATCHED AS WE DID IN HORROR
AS SIX DOZEN HUMANS BURNED IN HER RICHEST BOROUGH

70

PICTURE	PICTURE NOTHING
PICTURE	TIMELESS SPACE
PICTURE	THE BEGINNING
PICTURE	WHAT TO CREATE
PICTURE	PICTURE EMPTINESS
PICTURE	NO TIME NO SPACE
PICTURE	BEFORE CREATION
PICTURE	WITH WHAT TO MAKE
BANG	BANG GOES THE THEORY
BANG	IT'S ENERGY IT'S TIME

71

WHAT'S YOUR GAME
WHAT'S YOUR NAME
WHAT'S YOUR OPINION
IS IT THE SAME
THE WORLDS GONE MAD
THE WORLD IS BAD
THE WORLD IS SUFFOCATING
THIS IS SAD
OUR CARBON FOOTPRINTS OFF THE SCALE
YOU CAN'T GET A SEAT ON BRITISH RAIL
THERES MORE JET FUEL AND LESS ICE TO SEE
THE POLAR BEARS DROWNING IN A FISH LESS SEA
THE ASTRONAUT WEATHER MEN
AND COSMONAUTS BELIEVE
TIMES RUNNING OUT FOR POLAR BEARS YOU & ME
STOP LOOK & LISTEN TO THE BEAT OF THE DRUM
HEART BEATS STOP SILENCE THE GUNS

STOP THE BLOOD SHED OF ANIMALS
STOP THE BLOOD SHED OF HUMANS
STOP THE BLOOD BEING SHED
BY ALL THESE RELIGIOUS MEN
THEY READ THE W R O N G BOOKS
THEY ARE ALL A BUNCH OF CROOKS
CHARITIES OF CHURCHES
SYNAGOGUES AND MOSQUES
THEY DON'T PAY TAX
WE PAY THE PRICE
WE PAY THE PREACHERS
WITH OUR BLOODS & MONIES
WE ARE THE SACRIFICE

72

I WAS BORN A GENETIC JEW
BELIEVING IN JUDAISM
SO I READ ABOUT
ALL OTHER RELIGIONS
I NOW CHOOSE TO BE AN ATHEIST
TO YOU ESPECIALLY THE JEW
DOES THIS NOW MAKE ME
ANTI-SEMITIC

73

HARRY LESLIE SMITH
YOU SPOKE FOR ALL SOCIALISTS
YOUR SHOULDERS WE STAND ON
AS WE ALL RESIST
THE FASCIST TORY AUSTERITY
LAWFULLY IMPOSED ON US
POOR SOCIABLE SUBJECTS
BY THE FEW
IN THE GANG OF BLUES

74

ONE CANNOT SEE THE WOOD
FROM THE TREES CHOPPED DOWN
ONE CANNOT SEE THE METAL
FOR MACHINES TO THRIVE
ONE CANNOT SEE ANY POSITIVES
FROM THE NEGATIVE TORY RIDE
PEOPLE CAN SEE JEREMY CORBYN
RESTORE SOME SOCIAL PRIDE

75

DIM CITY LIGHTS
SHROUDED IN SMOG
GLIMMER AND SHIMMER
LIKE FLAMES ON A LOG
MASKED IN MIST
THAT ROLLS IN OFF THE SEA
RED AND YELLOW LIGHTS
GLEAM AND BECKON ME
THE CITY
LIGHTS THE HEARTS
OF THEATRE GOERS
MAKE LIGHT HEARTED
LAUGHTER
OF THE WEATHER
WHEREVER ONE GOES

76

NEWS PAPERS HAVE BEEN
INDEPENDENTLY PRODUCED
FOR OVER THREE HUNDRED YEARS
THE DAILY INDEPENDENT
IS THE FIRST TO GO DIGITAL
IS THIS THE BEGINNING OF THE END
OF THE PRINTED DAILY
NEWS PAPER AFTER ALL

77

POETRY COMMOTION
I COMPARE YOU TO A STAR
YOU ARE OH MY (A) CONSTELLATION
FOREVER SHINING FROM AFAR
POETRY COMMOTION
KNOWING YOU WHOM YOU ARE
I MAY NOT ALWAYS SEE YOUR PERFECTIONS
BUT AT NIGHT I KNOW WHERE YOU ARE
POETRY COMMOTION
OUT AMONGST BILLIONS OF STARS
I PICKED YOU OUT OF THE COMMOTION
SHINING BRIGHTER AND STRONGER
SO DEAR BY FAR

78

TO SEE AND NOT BE SEEN
IS TO HEAR AND NOT BE HEARD
SO TO NOT HEAR
AND HAVE BEEN HEARD
IS TO SPEAK AND
NOT HAVE SPOKEN
IS EQUALLY JUST ABSURD
SO SPEAK OF THAT
WHICH IS SPOKEN
AND MAKE SENSE
OF THE ABSURD

79

ONE HEARS ONE MUTTER
WE'RE ALL ONE STEP AWAY FROM THE GUTTER
DEBT ON A KNIFE EDGE
BALANCED UPON LIES
THE FINANCIAL MACHINE
TRUNDLES ON AS IT TRIES
TO EMULATE BUT HESITATES
MAKES SOME MISTAKES AND CRIES
WE'RE ALL DOOMED
WE'RE ALL IN DEBT
WE'RE ALL UP TO OUR EYES
THE LIES OF THE BANKERS
OUGHT TO BE TRIED
BUT THE TEARS OF THE BANKERS
ARE NEVER TO BE DRIED

80

IF I WAS A VISITING ALIEN
I'D FIND HUMANITY DESPICABLE
MYTHOLOGICAL INDIFFERENCES
POLITICAL DIVIDES
RACE APARTHEID
RICH AND POOR
NO PEACE
JUST WARS

81

JULIAN ASSANGE A POLITICAL PRISONER
A PRISONER OF THE STATE
IMPRISONED BY TORIES WESTERN POWERS
PERSECUTED BY THE UNITED STATES
THE WOMAN IN QUESTION
WHO SUPPOSEDLY CRIED RAPE
YEARS LATER CLAIMS THE POLICE
MADE IT UP A MISTAKE
NO EVIDENCE FOUND
BY ECUADOR INVESTIGATION
AND NONE FOUND BY
THE UNITED NATIONS

82

IT IS WELL KNOWN AND DOCUMENTED
THROUGHOUT THE WORLD
THAT THE UNITED STATES
EMERGENCY SERVICES NUMBER IS 911
SO WAS THE TWIN TOWERS DISASTER
IN SEPTEMBER 11 2001
MORE THAN A COINCIDENCE
TO COMMEMORATE FOREVER
9II AND NINE/ ELEVEN 2001

83

WE ENCOURAGE CHILDREN
TO TAKE UP SPORT
SAYING PARTICIPATING
IS THE END RESULT
CONTRARY TO THE FACT
WHEN PLAYING THEY'RE TAUGHT
YOU MUST WIN YOU MUST WIN
OR YOU'RE A LOOSER
FOOD FOR THOUGHT
COMPETITION IS NOT
THE BEST FORM OF TUITION
THE RESULTS ARE PROOF
OF THEIR FRUITION
ALL CLASSES AND GROUPS
SET TO COMPETE
THEY ARE ALL DOOMED LOSERS
EXCEPT ONE
THE ONLY LONELY ONE
WON

84

WE HAVE NO FAITH
WITH BELIEVERS AND THEIR BELIEFS
THEIR RELIGIOUS THOUGHTS
DO NOT EVOLVE
SCIENTIFICALLY SPEAKING
WE HAVE QUESTIONS SOLVED
IT IS TIME THE BELIEVERS
PROVED TO SCIENCE
GOD THE CREATOR OF ALL THINGS
EXISTS

85

CHASING MONEY
IS LIKE HENRY AND CHARLIE
BOTH THE TAIL AND THE HEAD
CIRCUMNAVIGATES THE END

86

WE ARE ALL VICTIMS OF
INDOCTRINATION
EDUCATION RELIGION
POLITICS AND SOCIAL MEDIA
CHOICE IS YOUR FREEDOM
CHOOSE REBIRTH BY
QUESTIONING ALL

87

DOWNING LILY THE PINK
DROWNING INSIDE WE THINK
DRAWING THE LINE IN THE SAND
CLENCHING THE BOTTLE IN HAND
QUENCHING THE THIRST
WHATEVER CAME FIRST
THE RETCHING
THE QUENCHING
IT ALL BLOODY HURTS

88

WHERE THERE'S WILL
THERE ARE WAYS
WHERE THERE IS A WILL
THERE IS A LAWYER

89

WHEN YOU SEE ME
LOOK UP TO THE SKY
IT WILL BE A HELICOPTER
A BIRD OR A FLY
IT MAY EVEN BE RAIN-DROPS
A PLANE PASSING BY
BUT IT WILL NEVER BE A GOD
WHO DOES NOT EXIST IN MY EYES

90

THE HIGH STREET IS DYING
LOBBY YOUR LOCAL COUNCIL & TOWN HALL
SURE PEOPLE SHOP ON LINE BUT THE BLAME LIES FIRMLY
WITH LOCAL FASCIST LAND LORDS

91

WHEN IS A JOURNALIST
NOT A JOURNALIST
WHEN THE JOURNALIST REPORTS THE
POLITICAL VIEWS OF THEIR RESPECTIVE BOSSES

92

WHEN IS A POLICEMAN
NOT A POLICEMAN
NEVER

93

TO UNLOCK SECRETS AND LOVE
WE ARE ALL BUT KEYS
TO UNLOCK SECRETS AND LOVE
HIDDEN DEEP WITHIN US ALL AS WE
SEARCH HIGH AND LOW AND
STAY OPEN TO ALL THINGS
NEEDING TO FIND THAT PARTNER / FRIEND
TO SET OURSELVES FREE

94

THE ENGLISH ROSE
ABOVE BIRD AND TREE
LABOURS SYMBOL
TO BE SOCIALLY
FREE

95

CLOUDS THAT MAKE FACES
TAKE ONE TO OTHER PLACES
THE SPACES BETWEEN
OFFER ALTERNATIVE DREAMS
LOST IMAGINATION
TRANSCENDS ONES RELATION
WITH REALITY QUESTIONED
CONSIDERATIONS AND ALTERATIONS
REVELATIONS OF TIME
LESS ANSWERS OF THE MIND
THE TEST OF THE QUEST
THAT CLOUDS OUTLINE AND DEFINE
DRIFTING FROM PLACES
THESE CLOUDS TAKE AWHILE
TO UNRAVEL THEIR MEANING
ALL CLOUD FACES SMILE
SAVE SEND OR DELETE

96

CREATIVITY

IS IN THE MIND OF THE BEHOLDER

97

WE WILL NOT MISS THE BIGOTS
THE SMALL MINDED BELIEVERS
THE PARANOID LAW MAKERS
NOR THE BANK EXECUTIVE GANGSTERS
THEIR EGOS PRIMED TO DELIVER
FEAR AND DEBT TO US ALL
THROUGH THE SYSTEM OF
GOD FEARING DEBT
TO KEEP US ALL DOWN TRODDEN
POOR SUBMISSIVE AND INERT

98

FICTIONAL STORIES
ARE IMAGINARY CHARACTERS AND EVENTS
LIKE FANTASIES ARE MAKE-BELIEVE AND
BELIEF IS BASED UPON MYTHOLOGY
AND MYTHS ARE ANCIENT RELIGIOUS STORIES
NEEDING NO PROOF NOR LOGIC

99

TALIBAN PROVERB
YOU HAVE THE CLOCKS
WE HAVE THE TIME
YOU NOW FACE THE CLOCKS
WE NOW WATCH THE TIME
SPACE STANDS STILL
HOURS RUSH BY
MINUTES OF HATE
SECONDS OF LOVE
FIRST WE MUST TALK
TOGETHER CONVERSE
YOU HAVE THE BOOKS
WE HAVE THE WORDS
LOVE LIVE LIFE
KILLING HATE ABSURD
FUTURES PAST
HISTORIC TOMORROWS
NOW IS THE TIME
FOR LOVE NOT SORROW

100

I FEEL SO HUMBLED AND HONOURED
TO HAVE LIVED ON MOTHER EARTH
WHILST ONE WAS STILL ABLE
TO BREATH IN RELATIVELY SPEAKING
FRESH AIR THROUGH HER TREES
ABSORBING METHANE GAS AND CO2s TOO
IN HER SEAS AND REFLECTING
SUN LIGHT OFF HER GLACIERS
TO HAVE SEEN AND WALKED
AMONGST HER WILD LIFE
ROAMING FREELY THROUGH AFRICA
TO HAVE WITNESSED
VAST RAIN FORESTS
AND GREEN PASTURES
SEPARATING LIVESTOCK AND ARABLE FIELDS
WHEN FOUR SEASONS WERE
STILL BEING EXPERIENCED
NORTH AND SOUTH OF THE EQUATOR
SEEING CORAL REEFS STILL LIVING
IN ALL THEIR COLOURFUL SPLENDOUR
BENEATH OUR BEAUTIFUL
BLUE OCEANS
BOUND BY THESE EXPERIENCES AND MEMORIES
I SHALL ENDEAVOUR TO EDUCATE AND
HELP MY FELLOW MAN TO APPRECIATE
MOTHER EARTH
IN ALL HER WONDER

101

HOW MANY MILLIONS WORK FOR THEIR POVERTY
PAYING MORE EARNING LESS IT IS PURGATORY
21st CENTURY CONSERVATISM
IS FOR THE RICH NOT THE POOR
TELL US SOMETHING NEW
JEREMYS SOCIALISM IS AT THE DOOR No 10

102

SOMETIMES ONE FEELS ROMANTIC
SOMETIMES ONE FEELS BEMUSED
SOMETIMES ONE FEELS AGITATED
BY OTHER PEOPLES POINTS OF VIEW

SOMETIMES ONE FEELS CREATIVE
SOMETIMES ONE FEELS IN THE MOOD
SOMETIMES ONE FEELS FRUSTRATED
BY OTHER PEOPLES ATTITUDES

SOMETIMES ONE FEELS LIFES COMPLICATED
SOMETIMES ONE FEELS LIFES SIMPLE
SOMETIMES ONE FEELS MOMENTARILY COMPLEXED
BY OTHER PEOPLES RESTRICTED VIEWS

SOMETIMES ONE FEELS ONES STRONG ENOUGH
SOMETIMES ONE FEELS ONES JUST A FOOL
SOMETIMES ONE FEELS SO HIGH ONE FORGETS
ONE'S FALLING IN LOVE AND HOPES
TO CHANGE ATTITUDES

103

Dr. EAMS
CLARIFY FOR ME
THE REASONS TO BE
HERE AT ALL IT SEEMS
YOUR NOT HERE AND
WE'RE NOT THERE
THIS IS ALL BUT
A BEAUTIFUL DREAM
THANK YOU Dr. EAMS

104

MONKEYS AND APPLES
NUTS AND SEEDS
DO NOT NECESSARILY
FALL OR JOURNEY FAR
FROM THE TREE

105

CONTRARY TO ALL BELIEFS
THIS INCLUDES ALL NATIONS
PEACE DOES NOT EXIST
WITH RELIGIOUS INDOCTRINATIONS
FREEDOM MAY ONLY BE GAINED
WHEN MANKIND QUESTIONS HUMAN KIND
ONLY THEN WILL ONE EVER ATTAIN
SOLACE PEACE OF MIND

106

COMPETITION MEANS
99% LOSE
COMPETITIVE EDUCATION MEANS
ONLY ONE COMES FIRST
TO COMPETE IN A RACE MEANS
THERE IS ONLY ONE WINNER
COMPETITIVENESS MEANS
ISOLATION FOR A FEW
AND EXCLUSION FOR THE MANY

107

THERES GOT TO BE A BETTER SOLUTION
FOR PEOPLES LIVING IN MISERY
THEY LIVE THEIR LIVES IN UTTER CONFUSION
WITH NO SENSE OF REALITY
THEY KEEP THE PEACE
WITH THEIR DIGNITY
THEY LAW ABIDE
WITH THEIR PRIDE
THEY NOW PROTEST AS SIGNATORIES
TO LABOUR THE LARGEST PARTY IN EUROPE
FOR THEY HAVE NOTHING
YES NOTHING TO HIDE

108

THERE WAS A WISE MAN
THERE WAS A HORSE MAN
THERE WAS A WITCH
ALL THREE BECAME EMBROILED
ONCE THEY HAD PITCHED IN
THEY ALL BITCHED
THE THREE CANNOT AGREE
THEY ALL AGREE TO DISAGREE
IT IS AS BAFFLING TO THEM
AS THE MYTHOLOGY

109

WHATEVER	WORDS	LAY	UNSPOKEN
WHATEVER	STORIES	LAY	UNSHARED
WHATEVER	MUSICS	LAY	UNPLAYED
WHATEVER	SONGS	LAY	UNSUNG
THE	FUTURE	WILL	UNFOLD
HER	STORIES	YET	UNTOLD

110

LAZY WEED KILLERS
IGNORANT AUTHORITIES
GLYPHOSATES POISONS
ALL OF US ON EARTHS SIMPLY ECO SYSTEM

111

TERRORISM
AND LOOK WHAT JOURNEY IT IS ON
THE PLAUSIBLE MUNDANE FACTS
THAT REALITY THROWS UP EVERY SECOND OF
EVERY MINUTE OF EVERY DAY AND
TURNED INTO A WOVEN TAPESTRY JOURNEY
THROUGH POETIC TIME AND SPACE
THIS IS HERS AND HIS STORY

112

WHEN THE WORLD IS WATCHING
FROM EVERY CONCEIVABLE
CAMERA LENS ON EARTH
AND IN SPACE
MAN ENACTING THE SAME
SAVAGERY AS MAN DID
THOUSANDS OF YEARS AGO
LOVE APPEARS
AS A BEACON OF HOPE

113

THERE ARE MORE
MOBILE PHONES
THAN LOOS
IN THE LAND OF
GURUS

114

MAN HAS SPENT AN OBSCENE
AMOUNT OF TIME SINCE IT BEGAN
IN THE OBSESSIVE BELIEF OF
A GOD CREATOR
TO WORSHIP TO AND PRAY TO
THE TIME WOULD HAVE BEEN
BETTER SPENT ON ALL LIFE
ON EARTH & ROBOTS

115

HE DREW HIS

GUN TODAY

AND THEN HE

HUNG IT UP

116

IN THE UNIVERSITY OF
PENNSYLVANIAS MUSEUM
RESIDE THE NIPPUR TABLETS
50 IN ALL KNOWN AS
THE BABYLONIAN TABLETS
TRANSLATED BY JUNE 14 1914
61 DAYS BEFORE WW2
THEY READ
NOAH NOT ADAM ATE
FROM THE TREE OF LIFE
IN THE GARDEN OF EDEN AND
NOAH IS BLAMED FOR THE
LOSS OF ETERNAL LIFE AND
A GARDENER CALLED
NUHU SAVES THE ANIMALS
AND ALL HUMAN LIVES
SO WHO AND WHERE
IS ADAM LET ALONE EVE

117

VOTE IS IT YOUR FIRST TIME
VOTE WITH YOUR CONSCIENCE
VOTE WITH YOUR MIND
VOTE FOR WHAT YOU FEEL IS RIGHT
VOTE WITH YOUR HEAD
VOTE WITH YOUR HEART
VOTE SO YOU CAN SLEEP AT NIGHT
VOTE FOR THE SICK
VOTE FOR THE HOMELESS
VOTE SO THEY ALL MAY BE HOUSED
VOTE FOR YOUR RUBBISH TO BE RECYCLED
VOTE FOR SOYA MILK INSTEAD OF COWS
VOTE FOR YOUR MPs TO BE PAID LESS
VOTE FOR THE PARTY THAT PERFORMS BEST
VOTE FOR THE EURO
VOTE FOR THE POUND
VOTE FOR THE FOX
VOTE FOR THE HOUND
VOTE FOR THE EARTH
VOTE FOR THE SKY
JUST BLOODY WELL VOTE
MANY HAVE DIED FOR YOUR
RIGHTS TO VOTE

118

MAKE YOUR OWN JOURNEY
MAKE YOUR OWN PATH
MAKE YOUR OWN STEPS
FORWARD FROM THE PAST

MAKE YOUR OWN TIME
MAKE YOUR OWN PLANS
MAKE YOUR OWN PEACE
WHILST YOU STILL CAN

MAKE YOUR OWN DECISIONS
MAKE YOUR OWN FRIENDS
MAKE YOUR OWN LOVE
BLOSSOM TO THE END

119

BELIEVE IN YOURSELF
IT IS YOUR WEALTH
DON'T BELIEVE IN
ANYTHING ELSE

120

WE ALL JUMP THROUGH LOOPS
THROUGHOUT OUR ADULT LIVES
THE RICH THOUGH JUMP THROUGH LOOPHOLES
DESIGNED FOR THEM TO SURVIVE

121

BSE AND CJD Oct 2018
HAVE REARED THEIR UGLY HEADS IN ABERDEENSHIRE
ONE PREDICTED THE 48 MONTH OLD BREEDING COW SYSTEM
WOULD FAIL
AND HERE WE ARE WITH BSE AND CJD
STILL IN THE FOOD CHAIN
WAGGING IT'S TAIL
PLANTS DON'T GO MAD
ONLY COWS AND HUMANS

122

PRIVACY SHOULD BE THE
PROVERBIAL
PINNACLE OF
PEACE FOR EVERY
PERSON ON THIS
PLANET SO ALL
PSYCHOS EVERYWHERE
PLEASE
PLEASE
PISS OFF

123

TEENAGE DREAMS
HIT YOU HARD
THEY STAY WITH YOU
THEY MEAN NO HARM
THEY'LL NEVER FADE
NEVER ALARM
IN FACT THEY MAYBE
YOUR LUCKY CHARM
IN MEMORY OF DJ JOHN PEEL 12 11 04

124

THE BRITISH ISLES OF IRONY
WHERE THE FEW PRIVILEGED REAP ALL
WATCH THE MANY WHO CREATE THE WEALTH
PAY IN TAXES LOW WAGES AND ILL HEALTH SERVICE

125

GAELIC
IS A LANGUAGE
NOT A LOAD OF
LECHEROUS HOMOSEXUALS

126

THE SENTIENCY THE KING OF THE JUNGLE
AND THE SAVANNAH HAS OF IT'S PREY
IS TO GO FOR IT'S JUGULAR VEIN
IT'S WIND PIPE AND THROAT
TO STOP IT'S PREY
ANY FURTHER UNNECESSARY PAIN

127

PAINTED HEROES PORTRAY OUR PAST
HEROINE GODS OF WAR LAST
CHARACTERISTIC VIEWS OF WAR
RELIGIOUS TRAITS OF POWER HOUSE LAW
NEOLITHIC STONE AGE MAN
DRAWN IN TIME AND SPACE BY HAND
PICTURES STATE THEIR CODED PAST
PICTURE ME WITH SATELLITE MAST
FIND A NEW CHANNEL

128

WHAT HARMS THE WORTH OF A NATION ARE TAX DODGERS
LIKE THE BILLIONAIRE HARMSWORTH OWNER OF THE MAIL

129

ONE FEELS VACUUMED
BUT AT LEAST ONES CLEAN
ONE FEELS USED ABUSED
ONE EVEN FEELS CHEWED
ONE FEELS WASTED TASTED
ONE EVEN FEELS HATRED
ONE HAS GIVEN THEIR ALL
ONE HAS GIVEN THEIR BALLS
TO ALL AND SUNDRY
ONE DOES NOT SUFFER FOOLS
NOW ONE FEELS FREE
ONE FEELS EMPTY
EMPTIED OF ALL THEIR CONTEMPORARIES
ONE FEELS VACUUMED
BUT AT LEAST ONE IS CLEAN

130

BREEZES AND SUNSHINE
BREATHING IN AIR
FRESH SUMMER FLOWERS
THAT SPRING LEFT WITH CARE
WARM DAYS AND TULIPS
THAT COLOUR YOUR HAIR
IT'S SUMMER IN SPRING TIME
IT'S LOVE THAT I DEAR
MORE THAN PLACES WITH LACES
OF ATOMIC MEANS
OF SURVIVING THE DYING
OF MOTHERS OWN NEEDS

IF THE RACES KEEP PACES
IT'S LITTLE I DREAM
WHEN ITS SUMMER
IN SPRING TIME
IT'S LOVE THAT I BEAM
SEEING SHADES UNDER BRANCHES
THE SHADOWS OF SEEDS
NOW GROWN WITH SUMMERS
THEY ARE TALLER THAN ME
FORESTS OF TOPPERS
AND GREEN BELTS WITH STREAMS
OF LOVE IN THE SPRING TIME
AND MID SUMMER DREAMS

131

THERES A PEACE IN THE PLACE
WHERE YOU WASHED THE OTHER DAY
A PEACE OF LOVE ON A STONE
THERES THE CAT SAT ON THE MAT
WITH MY LOVE POISED WITH PLAITS
PAINTING PICTURES OF
FACELESS SCULPTURES ON A STONE
AND WHEN ALL NIGHTS ARE THROUGH
BEING AWAY FROM YOU
I WILL BE WITH YOU
TILL THEN MY LOVE GROWS
KEEP A SONG IN YOUR HEART
WHILST WE ARE APART
WE WILL KEEP SINGING
OUR SONG OF LOVE

132

WIND AND RAIN BLOW ON THE SCREEN
SNOWS APPEARING IN THE BEAM
IS THIS A MOVIE OR IS THIS A CAR
WHO IS THE DRIVER WHO IS THE STAR
WHAT WAS THAT WHAT IS THIS
A NOISE A SOUND AN AUDIO HISS
SOMETHINGS HUMMING IS IT A WHINE
SOUNDS LIKE THUNDER FROM BEHIND
LIFES JUST PASSING GIVE IT SOME TIME
WITHIN WITHOUT LOVE
THERES DOUBT NO HOPE
NO REASON ONLY APPEASEMENT
TURN OFF SLOW DOWN
SWITCH OFF NO SOUND
SOUNDS LIKE THUNDER
GET YE BEHIND
LIFES JUST PASSING SO GIVE IT SOME TIME

133

AREN'T THERE ANY
STRAIGHT BANANAS

134

IN WALES
THEY'VE GIVEN UP
KEEPING UP
WITH THE JONESES
RATHER QUOTE
THOMAS KEATS
YATES & BURNS

135

ATHEISTS
HAVE NO EXPECTATIONS

136

PAIN NO GAIN
WHO THOUGHT UP
THAT BLOODY NAME
IT'S NO GAME
IT'S A SHAME
PAIN IS PAIN
DO YOU ENJOY
EATING BRAINS
ANIMALS BRAINS
ANIMALS PAIN
IT'S NO DIFFERENT
TO OURS
PAIN IS THE SAME
BITE YOUR OWN ARM
BBQ IT RARE I GUESS
WHAT WILL IT TAKE
FOR YOU TO DIGEST
THERE IS NO GAIN
FROM ANY ANIMALS PAIN
ONLY ONES DIGESTION
OF EATING ANIMALS
QUESTION

137

ONE WANTS TO FINISH WHAT ONE HAS STARTED
ONLY TO FIND ONE HAS FARTED

138

THERE IS A GEYSER
UNDER A LIGHTHOUSE IN THE SKY FOREVER ON
IT'S IN QUEBEC CANADA
BUILT BY YOKO ONO LENNON FOR JOHN

139

I'D LOVE A JAR OF
JEREMYS JAM
ON TOAST WITH A CUPPA
WATCHING ARSENAL WEST HAM

140

VEGETARIANS ARE
JUST FUSSY CARNIVORES
WITH A CONSCIENCE
EVOLVING
STOP THE TORTURE
AND SLAUGHTER OF
ALL ANIMALS
DYING

141

REMEMBER
WHEN DODGING A BULLET
IT'S ALREADY BEEN FIRED

142

THE WEALTH OF A NATION
IS THE HEALTH OF THEIR CHILDREN
STOP EATING ANIMALS
AND THEIR BI PRODUCTS
DAIRY EGGS AND
ANYTHING WITH A FACE
THE FUTURE LIES IN
FRONT OF OUR EYES
SEIZE THE MOMENT
AND EMBRACE

143

VEGANS LOVE ANIMALS
THEY DON'T EAT ANYTHING
WITH A FACE

144

MOST PEERS APPEAR
UTTERLY DETERMINE
YET THEY ARE VERMIN
DRAPED IN ERMINE

145

F A I T H
THE PROCESS OF NON THINKING

146

VEGETABLES
DON'T *FART!*

147

HE LOOKED IN THE BOOK
HIS HEAD HE SHOOK
THE COOK PULLED A HOOK
FROM THE FISH TO COOK
BUT THE HOOK GOT MISTOOK
AND WAS TAKEN BY A ROOK
THAT FLEW IN AND TOOK
THE HOOK FROM THE COOK
WHO WROTE IN THE COOK'S BOOK
THE ROOK TOOK THE HOOK
Signed THE COOK
THE POLICEMAN CLOSED HIS BOOK
HIS HEAD SHOOK
AS HE GAVE THE LOOK
WAS IT THE CURTAIN HOOK
WAS IT BLACK BEARDS HOOK
WAS IT THE CAPTAINS HOOK
LOOK
IT'S IN THE BOOK
IT WAS THE ROOK
WHO TOOK THE HOOK
Signed THE COOK
IT COULD HAVE BEEN WORSE YOU KNOW
THE SILENCE TURNED TO SURPRISE
AS THEY ALL LEANED IN
TO HEAR THE POLICEMAN GRIN
IT COULD HAVE BEEN A CROOK
tune in next time to hear
POLICE LINES
Solved or Unsolved

148

MIRROR MIRROR
WHEN ONE'S ASKING
WHERE'S MY BEAUTY
IS THERE NOTHING
ON REFLECTION
WHAT IS YOUR
PERCEPTION
IS IT CLEAR OPAQUE
TRANSPARENT
OR CRACKED
IS THERE SOME REASON
WHY YOUR LOOKING BACK
TURN OVER TURN ROUND
LOOK TRUE AND STRAIGHT
LOOK INTO THE EYES
FACE TO FACE
MIRROR MIRROR
IT IS TRUE WHAT THEY SAY
I LAUGH WITH YOU AS YOU
LAUGH WITH ME
TOUSCHEZ

149

THE PAPAL PONTIFF PONCE
WHO PROUDLY POSES PUBLICLY AS POPE
PONDERS ONTO THE PODIUM PATIENTLY
PURPOSELY WE SUPPOSE
SPEAKING TO HIS DISCIPLES
HIS FLOCK A MASS OF CHILDREN
DRAFTED IN FROM FAR AWAY
BUMS ON SEATS FOR THE POPE
THE MAJORITY OF PEOPLE THEN
IN THE YEAR
TWO THOUSAND AND TEN
WE HEARD THEM SAY
WE WANT THE PONTIFF TO PAY
FOR HIS PAPAL HOLIDAY
HERE IN THE UK
HURRAH HURRAH
HE IS GONE
BANG A DRUM
BANG A GONG
PLEASE PLEASE
SING ALONG
THE PAPAL
PONTIFF POSE
HAS GONE

150

IF YOU FELL IN LOVE WITH PEACHES
YOU WOULD CHANGE YOUR NAME TO CREAM
IF YOU FELL IN LOVE WITH ULRIKA
YOU WOULD CRY EUREKA
IF YOU FELL IN LOVE WITH PARIS
YOU WOULD CALL YOURSELF
FRANC OF THE RITZ
BUT YOU FELL IN LOVE WITH CHAMPAGNE
AND HAVE STAYED FOREVER PISSED

151

AFRICA STILL STARVES
HUNDREDS OF YEARS PASS
AND STILL WE STRIVE FOR THE STARS
RELIGION STILL SHACKLES
MANKIND TO THE PAST
YET WE STILL STRIVE FOR THE STARS

152

MONEY FLOWS FOREVER THROUGH OUR POCKETS
PRINTING BREAD TO FEED THE RICH MANKIND PROFITS

153

SEND ME A TEXT OR A TWITTER SEE

I'LL BE DRIVING PAST IN YOUR VICINITY

I CAN PICK YOU UP WHEREVER YOU LIKE

BUT I'M NOT IN A CAR I'M ON A BIKE

154

SIRENS AND GUN SHOTS

WOMEN CRY AND MEN FLOP

PLANES FLY AND BOMBS DROP

ROCKETS WHIZZ AND MORTARS OFF

BLASTS AND CRASHES

BULLETS PING

THROUGH EERIE SILENCE

THEN nothing

155

TIME STANDS STILL
WHEN YOU WALK IN A ROOM
ELEGANCE TRANSCENDS YOUR SMILE
YOU LEAVE LIKE A PERFUME
YOU GLIDE LIKE A SWAN ON WATER
YOUR NECK TURNS AND MAKES YOU TALLER
LEGS LIKE A BALLERINA
MELANCHOLY LOOKS MAKES YOU SERENE
TIMELESS STILLS
WHEN YOU TALK YOU CHANGE THE MOOD
EVERYONE HANGING ONTO YOUR EVERY WORD
SILENTLY LISTENING TO A SONG BIRD
TIME STANDS STILL
YOUR ELEGANTLY DRESSED TO KILL
ONE WONDERS WHETHER WE EVER WILL BE
LOCKED IN LOVE
AS TIME STOOD STILL

156

I AM A PLYNTHIAN
A PLYNTHIAN I AM
A PERSON WHO HAS
PLYNTHED ON A PLINTH
WITH NO OTHER PERSON AROUND
WE PLYNTHIANS HAVE IN COMMON
THE FAMOUSLY THIRD AND VACANT PLYNTH
ON TRAFALGAR SQUARE OCCUPIERS FOR ONE HOUR
WHERE WE ALL BECAME PLYNTHIANS DON'T YOU THINK

157

BELIEF CAN'T BE BOMBED
RAPED SHOT OR STOPPED
HYPNOTISED
RELIGIONS THE TOOLS
FOR MULES AND FOOLS
SUICIDE

158

IF MUSIC BE
THE FOOD OF LOVE
YOU'RE MY RECIPE

159

I WILL REMEMBER YOUR FACE
AND YOUR SMILE
I WILL REMEMBER YOUR HUMOUR
FOR A WHILE
I WILL REMEMBER YOUR STYLE
EVEN IF YOUR VAIN
BUT DON'T EXPECT ME TO
REMEMBER YOUR NAME

160

ONE REMEMBERS THE 50's
IN BLACK AND WHITE
ONE REMEMBERS THE 60's
PSYCHEDELIC & BRIGHT
ONE REMEMBERS THE 70s
GLAM ROCK TO PUNK
THE 80s ROMANTICS
DJ's AND GARAGE
RAPPERS & RAVERS
HIP HOP 90s & ROCKAGE
MILLENNIUM FEVER
THE NAUGHTIES HAVE ARRIVED
MUSIC GENRES & STYLES
ALL DIGITALISED

161

VICTIMLESS CRIME
GETTING DRUNK Oh NO WHY
SMOKING SKUNK GETTING HIGH
SELF HARMING Oh NO WHY
EAT TO OBESE OR PUKE BULIMIC
VICTIMLESS CRIME
WHY Oh WHY Oh WHY

162

IN THE SURGERY OF THE DOCTOR
YOUR HEALTH IS IN THEIR HANDS
AS HUMBLE AS WE ALL ARE
WE TRY AND UNDERSTAND
THEIR DIAGNOSIS IS CRITICAL
ON EXPLANATION OF OUR
SYMPTOMS
AS FAR AWAY WITH THEIR STARE
YOU FEEL TRANSPARENTLY SIMPLE
THROUGH FURTHER INVESTIGATION
ON EXAMINATION OF THESE EVENTS
YOU ARE LEFT WITH
THE VAGUE SYNOPSIS
YOU MAY OR MAY NOT
BE DEAD

163

IT DEPENDS ON THE QUESTION
WHAT ANSWER ONE GIVES
IT DEPENDS ON THE QUESTION
BEING RELATIVE TO ME
WE DEPEND ON EACH OTHER
BEING INDEPENDENT AND FREE
TO ANSWER THE QUESTION
SO DEPENDENT ON WE

164

MY INQUISITION IS OVER
I AM RELINQUISHED OF ALL MY DOUBTS
BY MY SOLICITORS WHOM INFORMED ME
AND THEY AGREED THAT
I'VE BEEN MEDICALLY OVERDOSED
BY QUACKS

165

ONE CAN SEE THE LIGHT AT THE END
OF THE EURO BREXIT TUNNEL
BUT WHICH WAY IS ONE LOOKING

166

I BELIEVE GENETICALLY
IN THE D N A OF WE
HUMAN BEINGS
EVOLVING FROM MICROBIOLOGY
I BELIEVE SCIENTIFICALLY
IN THE WORLD AROUND ME
AS IT REVOLVES
WE EVOLVE AUTOMATICALLY
I MUST THEREFORE BELIEVE
THERE ARE NO PEARLY GATES
NO DOORS NO FENCES
NO BARBED WIRE NO STATES
NO ILLUSIONS
NO ETHEREAL PLACE EXISTS
LOVE HAS NO RESTRICTIONS
LOVE IS EXQUISITE

167

SOMETHING WENT BANG AND IT HIT ME
NO ONE HAS EVER PROVED TO ME
THAT THERE IS A GOD
LOVE WAS TAUGHT AND PROVED TO ME
THROUGH MY FAITHFUL DOG
THE EVER FLOWING
SHOWERING EFFECT OF RELIGIONS
EXISTS LIKE A FOG
WHILST THE PEOPLE ON EARTH
TURN SLOWLY TO SCIENCE
THE WORLD TURNS SLOWLY
IN THE UNIVERSE JUST A MERE COG
SOMETHING WENT BANG
THE UNIVERSE BEGAN
AND LIFE AS WE KNOW IT
ROSE LIKE A PHOENIX FROM THE LAND
LOVE RESPECT CARE AND COMPASSION
RESIDES IN EACH AND EVERYONE OF US
WITH A PASSION
SOMETHING WENT BANG AND IT HIT ME

168

ALL MEN CAN GROW BEARDS
SOME CHOOSE NOT TO
THE BAIRD OR THE BEARD
THIS IS THE QUESTION

169

I THINK I FAST I WAIT
I CONTEMPLATE
THE MEANING OF LIFE
AND LOVE AND HATE
PICTURES OF SELF
WEALTH AND POVERTY
WARS OF THE SEXES
LET ALONE RELIGIONS
1st CLASS UPPER CLASS
LOWER CLASS OUTCAST
THE PRESENT FUTURE
THE MEMORIAL PAST
LOVE AND FRIENDSHIP
TRUST AND RESPECT
LIES AND ABUSE
I DO NOT ACCEPT

170

I'M OBVIOUSLY AN ATHEIST
BECAUSE OF THE FACTS
A 1st CENTURY BOOK WRITTEN WHEN
THEY THOUGHT THE WORLD WAS FLAT
THIS COMPILATION OF STORIES
HAVE NEVER BEEN PROVED
SCIENTIFICALLY SPEAKING
ALL CHARACTERS MAYBE TABOO
HAS ANYONE LATELY EVER READ
THE WHOLE BLOODY BOOK
ITS BARBARIC IMMORAL & RACIST
TAKE A LOOK AT THIS BOOK

IF I TAKE ME A WIFE
AND A VIRGIN SHE IS NOT
I MAY STONE HER TO DEATH
OUTSIDE HER FATHERS HOUSE
AND THAT WILL BE HER LOT

BLASPHEMY HEARSAY
AN IMAGINARY CRIME
THEY ARE STILL STONED TO DEATH
TIME AFTER TIME
ISLAM JUDAISM CHRISTIANITY
THE THREE MAIN ACTS
THE OTHER TWO BOOKS
FULL OF THE SAME CRAP

171

OFF THE RAILS
WE'RE ALL OFF THE RAILS
WALKING IN SUMMER SUITS
AUTUMN COATS WINTER BOOTS
SPRING INTO FASHION
BECAUSE THE FUTURE LOOKS GOOD
THE COLOUR OF YOUR MONEY
WILL MASK THE COLOUR OF YOU

172

PRICELESS FREEDOM
WHEN EDUCATION GIVES YOU AWAY
PRICELESS FREEDOM
WHEN RELIGION GIVES YOU AWAY
PRICELESS FREEDOM
WHEN D N A GIVES YOU AWAY
PRICELESS FREEDOM
WHEN YOU YOURSELF STAY SHUT AWAY
PRICELESS HUMAN RIGHTS
WHEN WE STAND AND UNITE
PRICELESS FREEDOM

173

BRITAIN INVENTED THE CHAMPAGNE BUBBLES
IN THE 16th CENTURY FROM
GINGER BEER CULTURE
FRANCE FOUNDED THE CAGED CORK MUCH LATER
CHAMPAGNE FROM CHAMPAGNE BREWED
WITH BRITISH CULTURE

174

VIRGIN SOLDIERS
CIVILIANS AND NUNS
MONKS AND LAMAS
IN FACT ANY HUMANS
ESCAPING THE DIRT
DISHED OUT BY LIFE
SOMEDAY ITS GOING TO STICK
WHILST LIFE PASSES BY
YOU WONT ESCAPE THE FEELING
OF HOPELESSNESS NO HOPE
NO WAY OF KNOWING
HOW MANY BARS OF SOAP
IT TAKES TO STAY CLEAN
FROM LIFE'S MACHINE
CHEWING THE DIRT
AND ALL FILTH THATS NOT CLEAN
LIFE'S PLEASURES AND BEAUTY
SWIRL LIKE A SHROUD
EXISTING IN THE BUBBLES
OF DREAMS MAKING CLOUDS
AND WHILST THE BUBBLES FORM
THEN BURST ANOTHER IS SHED
SO TOO ANOTHER DREAM EXISTS
INSIDE SOMEONES HEAD
WHO IN TURN TELLS SOMEONE
OF THE THOUGHT THEY HAD
AS THE CORK LEAVES THE BOTTLE
OF BUBBLING CHAMPAGNE
I T BEGINS WITH A SPLISH
TO ANOTHER IT'S A SPLASH
AND THAT'S HOW I'D
LIKE TO LEAVE IT
WITH JUST A DASH -

175

WISPY CLOUDS UP IN THE SKY
THEY DON'T SEEM TO MOVE
THEY LOOK VERY HIGH
THERE ARE CARS PASSING
ON THE FREEWAY
IT'S GETTING DARK AND RAINING
IN THE DISTANCE THEY SEEM TO FADE AWAY
THEIR LIGHTS AT NIGHT STREAM PASS LIKE TRAINS
THERE AGAIN A LONE CAR STICKS OUT IN THE RAIN

176

WHEN YOU OPEN YOUR MOUTH
WORDS UTTER OUT
THEY ARE NEITHER A MURMUR
NOR ARE THEY A SHOUT
WHENEVER YOU MUTTER
OR MURMUR OR EVEN POUT
JUST OPEN YOUR MOUTH
AND LET THE BLOODY WORDS OUT

177

I THINK YOUR BRAVE
AND COURAGEOUS
STANDING OUT THERE
IN THE COLD
I THINK YOUR STRENGTH
IS CONFRONTATIONAL
IN FRONT OF POLICE LINES
SO BOLD
I BELIEVE YOUR CONSCIOUS COMMITMENT
IN JUST STANDING AT WILL
STARING OUT POLICE LINES
SO COLD SO BRAVE SO STILL

178

PERHAPS
HE CAME FROM THE GUTTERS OF DESPERATION
CRAWLING OUT OF THE MYRE
LEFT BY MOODS OF DEPRESSION
FISCAL PENNY PINCHER
PIMPS OF THE STREET
WHERE A PERSONS PRIVILEGE IS
PERMANENTLY PINCHED
PUNCH DRUNK AND PUKING
PREFERABLY PISSED
PASS ALL THE POSERS WHO PERFORM
AS HE PERCHED PROUDLY
PRONOUNCING A sPeCiFiC PieCe
PARALYTIC AND PALE HE
PASSED AWAY PEACEFULLY
PERHAPS?

179

ONE SHOULD BE GLAD ONES NOT A TURKEY
AT CHRISTMAS TIME AT LEAST
ONE SHOULD BE GLAD ONES NOT A COW
COMING UP TO THE AGE OF FOUR
ONE SHOULD BE GLAD ONES NOT A PIG
A GOAT A DUCK OR A SHEEP
I'M JUST GLAD THAT I'M A VEGAN
AND I AM ABLE TO WEEP
AND SLEEP

180

CARS ARE GREAT TO RIDE DRIVE OR BASH
THEY ARE SO COOL ESPECIALLY WHEN THEY CRASH
JUMPING WITH JOY WE LOVE TO RIDE
AND PLAY ON THE SWINGS BETTER STILL THE SLIDE
SHOES AND DINOSAURS
MOON AND STARS
THESE WERE YOUR FIRST WORDS
SHOE MOON AND STARS
BUT IT WAS DINOSAURS
THAT REALLY MADE US LAUGH

181

HOW CAN ONE TAKE A BEAR
CAGE IT AND TRAIN IT
TO BEG ON A CHAIN
TO THE TUNE OF HIS PAIN
SO TRANSLUCENTLY PLAIN
HE MUST BE UNCHAINED AND
GIVEN HIS FREEDOM AGAIN

182

HOW CAN WE BE EXPECTED
TO ELECT OUR LEADERS
WHO HAVE AND NEED NO CREDENTIALS
TO LEAD AND GOVERN OUR COUNTRY
TO BE AN ENGINEER OR A HAIRDRESSER
PHYSICIAN OR LAWYER
ONE NEEDS TO PASS EXAMINATIONS
AFTER YEARS OF STUDIES AND APPLICATIONS
OF THEIR SKILLS CRAFTS & PROFESSIONS
IN THE BUSINESS WORLD
TO OBTAIN THOSE PIECES OF PAPER
PROCLAIMING ONES DIPLOMA

183

THINK OF ALL THE TIMES
YOU SAID NO
WHEN YOU OUGHT TO
HAVE LET GO
REMEMBER THE TIMES
YOU DID LET GO
THE TIMES YOUR GLAD
YOU DIDN'T SAY NO

184

WHEN ONE AWAKES
ONE CAN'T ESCAPE
THE FEELING THAT
ITS PROBABLY LATE
FAKE OR STRAIGHT
MATES ARE GREAT
FOR GOODNESS SAKE
EARLY OR LATE
DON'T MAKE THE MISTAKE
YOUR NEVER TOO EARLY AND
LATE IS WELL TOO LATE
BETTER LATE THAN NEVER
BUT NEVER SAY NEVER BECAUSE
NEVER EVER SEEMS TO COME AT ALL

185

I'M MINIMALLY BRADY KINETIC
WITH A MOST DELIGHTFUL SWAY
CENTURIES & CENTURIES OF ABUSE
IN A FRIGHTFULLY GENETIC WAY

186

HE'D DONE IT ALL BEFORE BREAKFAST
BEFORE SEVEN BEFORE HE WAS SEVEN
CLIMBED THE SPHINX
MADE OF SANDS THAT WERE ONCE EVEN
SLIDE OVER GLACIERS WITH PENGUINS & SEALS
BUILT SHELTERS IN THE WOODLANDS
AND BOATS FOR THE SEAS
OR STOP YOUR IMAGINATION
AND WATCH IT ON SOME SCREEN

187

I SAT BY 'MUFF' WHO TREMBLED WITH TOUCH
SHE LOOKED WELL ENOUGH WE'LL MISS HER MUCH
HER PAIN YOU COULD SEE AS SHE LAY DISEASED
SHE BLINKED IT'S NOT A WINK
SHE WAS SEEING BLINKING SHADOWS
HER EARS AND HER MOUTH
MUST OF MADE HER WANT TO SHOUT
SHE LOOKED SO BEAUTIFUL DRINKING MILK
FUCK I'M GOING TO MISS
NOT HAVING MUFF ABOUT
I'LL NEVER BE INTERRUPTED IN A FILM AGAIN
I'LL NEVER HAVE TO WALK HER IN THE FLIPPING RAIN
I'LL NEVER HAVE THAT PLEASURE AGAIN
OF SWIMMING WITH HER IN THE SEA
OR WALKING IN THE WOODS OR ALONG THE SANDS
JUST LIKE IT USED TO BE

188

WHERE ARE ALL THE HIPPIES
WHERE ARE ALL THEIR KIDS
WHERE ARE ALL THEIR PHILOSOPHIES
THEIR MORALS WE ALL MISS
WHERE ARE ALL THE FLOWERS
THAT HAVE EVER BEEN SENT
TO MARK THE GRAVES OF
ALL OTHER CHILDREN SENT
TO WARS TO PREVENT

189

AS PURE AS WATER FALLS
IT RAINS
AS TRUE AS A CHILDS LOVE
IS CERTAIN
AS CLEAR AS DAYLIGHT SHINES
YOU'LL SMILE
AS DEAR AS A BIRD IN FLIGHT
IS FREE FOR A WHILE

190

ONE HAS NO CAR BUT ONE LOVES TO DRIVE
ONE HAS NO PLANE YET ONE LOVES TO FLY
ONE TAKES THE TRAIN TO EASE THE STRAIN
OR A BALLOON OR A FEW JUST FOR THE FUN
LOOK OUT THE WINDOW
WHERE WHICH ONE
ANYONE THE NEAREST
CAN YOU SEE THE SUN
WHAT DO YOU SEE MAYBE THE MOON
CLOUDS BLUE SKY
AT NIGHT NAVY BLUE
IN DAYLIGHT IS THERE A GARDEN
FULL OF YELLOW DAFFODILS
OR IF YOUR IN THE CITY MORES THE PITY
MAYBE YOU SEE ONLY
RUDDY GREAT RED BRICK WALLS

191

LET US BE CLEAR ACKNOWLEDGE AND STATE
THE REALITY SHOW STAR DONALD TRUMP
THE PRESIDENT OF THE UNITED STATES
HAS ADDRESSED THE ASSEMBLY OF THE UNITED NATIONS
IN NEW YORK AND ACCLAIMING
SOCIALISM DEPRIVES FINANCIAL REWARDS
AND LEADS TO POVERTY
WHEREVER IT REARS ITS UGLY HEAD
AND WHEN THE 21st CENTURIES MOST FASCIST LEADER TO DATE
ANNOUNCED THAT HE AND HIS TEAM
HAD ACHIEVED MUCH MORE IN THEIR TIME IN OFFICE
HE WAS MET WITH VERY SLOW HAND CLAPS
AND LOUD MOCKING LAUGHTER

192

OK GOOGLE
HOW MANY HOMELESS PEOPLE HAVE YOU HOUSED
NONE
IF YOU PAID YOUR STATUTORY TAXES ANNUALLY
YOU COULD HOUSE THEM ALL
PLUS ONE

193

COME IN A CAB
COME IN A TRAIN
COME IN A HELICOPTER
COME IN A PLANE
COME IN YOUR SHOES
COME IN YOUR BOOTS
COME IN YOUR A LAUGH
COME IN YOUR A HOOT
COME IN A HAT
COME IN A COAT
COME IN A CAR
COME IN A BOAT
COME IN A BUS
COME IN ON A BIKE
COME IN A PERAMBULATOR
COME IN ANYTHING YOU LIKE
COME IN FROM THE COLD
COME IN FROM THE FACTORY
COME IN FROM THE LAND
COME IN FROM THE COUNTRY
COME IN FROM THE RAIN
COME IN FROM THE SNOW
COME IN FROM THE WEATHER
COME IN YOU NEVER KNOW
COME IN FOR AWHILE
COME IN FOR A CHAT
COME IN FOR A SMILE
COME IN FOR A NAP
COME IN IF YOUR UGLY
COME IN IF YOUR CUTE
COME IN EVERYONE IN ANYTHING OR NOTHING
COME IN YOUR BIRTHDAY SUIT

194

TIME MACHINE GENE
IS IN EVERY LIVING THING
BY THE MOON AND THE SUN
TO THE STARTING PISTOL GUN
TIME IS THE SEASONS
THEY RETURN EVERY ONE
A CYCLE A SYSTEM
A REPETITIVE REASON
OF PROCESS AND MOTION
PRODUCING PRODUCING
TIME IS EVERLASTING
TIME IS EVERYTHING
SO WHAT DO YOU WANT
CHOICE OR INSTINCT
TIME IS INVISIBLE
TIME IS UNTOUCHABLE
TIME IS PERSONAL
TIME IS A TIME MACHINE GENE

195

WHOS AN ALCOHOLIC
WHO DRINKS WINE
NOT ME
WHO PREFERS A NIP HERE & THERE
A DRINK AFTER LUNCH AND BEFORE TEA
ITS JUST A LITTLE DRINK
JUST ONE FOR THE ROAD
AND MAYBE JUST ANOTHER
ALRIGHT THEN YOU ROGUE
ITS JUST A LITTLE DRINK
JUST ONE MORE FOR
YoU SiR eR OR Sir eR
AN ALCOHOLICS LIFE IS NOT TO BE DESIRED

196

VISUALISATION
RAILWAY STATION
TICKETS TO RIDE
WHEREVER YOU MENTION
VISUALISE RAIN IF YOU CAN
VISUALISATION
MARIJUANA PLANTATION
MONEY FOR OLD ROPE
FOR THE POPULATION
VISUALISE RAINBOWS IF YOU CAN
VISUALISATION
ATOMIC REGENERATION
HOME PODS FOR SALE
ANY SIZE AND DESTINATION
VISUALISE SUNSHINE IF YOU CAN
VISUALISATION
CLIMATICAL REALISATION
CLIMATE CHANGE REVELATIONS
RADIATION
VISUALISE SNOW FALLING IF YOU CAN

197

WALLS DO NOT IMPRISON MATES
WALLS MANAGE ONLY TO SEPARATE
MALES FROM FEMALES
WARDENS FROM INMATES
WALLS AND CELLS ALL IMPRISONED
FOR WHOSE SAKE

198

NOT SINCE THE 1960s 70s
HAS ANY NORTHERN WESTERN COUNTRY
BEEN ALLOWED TO DREAM
WITNESSING THE POWER OF LOVE
FREEDOM OF SPEECH & MANPOWER STRIKES
THE HIPPIES PROVED
WARS CAN BE STOPPED
DREAMS CAN BE FULFILLED
WELCOME TO 21st CENTURY REALITY
FAKE FRAUD FICTION AND FEUDS

199

DOCTORS AGAINST DESTRUCTION & DISEASE
DEDICATED & DRIVEN BY DESIRE TO DELIVER
EARTHS MOST NATURAL REMEDIES
WITH MANS MOST ADVANCED MEDICAL TECHNOLOGIES

200

SILENTLY YOU WAIT
FOR THE TURN OF A KEY
THE CLICK OF THE DOOR
THE RUSTLE OF A COAT
YOU SIT QUIETLY
SMOKING A CHEROOT
YOUR EYES OPEN
TENDERLY YOU LOOK
NO WORD OF MOUTH
NO BECKONING HAND
THE EYES JUST STARE
IN A SILENT COMMAND
ARMS STRETCHED OUT
COAT ON FLOOR
EMBRACE THE SILENCE

201

ONES THINKING OF OTHERS

AS ONE LOOKS AT THE SCREEN

LOOK AT THE PICTURE

OF A 50 KILO DART

PIERCING THE SKIN OF A

MINKE WHALES HEART

WHAT MAKES MAN FEEL

HE HAS THE RIGHT

TO KILL AND EAT ANY OTHER CREATURE

ON EARTH INCLUDING HUMAN LIFE

KILLING WHALES IS MURDER

THE SAME AS KILLING ONES WIFE

WHALES HAVE THE RIGHT FOR LIFE

202

DON'T RUIN IT
DON'T SAY ANYTHING
DON'T MISS THE MOMENT
LIVE THE MOMENT
IT MEANS EVERYTHING
STOP LOOK AND LISTEN
OUR HEARTS BEAT TO THE DRUM
LIVE LIFE TO THE FULL
STAY HOT BUT LOOK COOL
AND BE NOBODY'S FOOL
LIFE IS WORTH LIVING
WHETHER YOUR RICH OR POOR
THERES NO GETTING AWAY
THERES ONLY ONE LIFE SO HEY
LET'S GIVE LIFE
ONE MORE DAY
UNLESS TODAY'S THE DAY

203

WORLD WIDE WEAVERS OF THE WEB IN QUESTION
ANSWERS ARE THE QUEST
INFO TECHNO NANO SYSTEMS
QUESTIONS ARE THE BEST
WHEN ANSWERED

204

I DON'T SWIM WITH THE REST OF THEM
AND THEY DON'T SWIM WITH ME
I DON'T SING THE SAME SONGS AS THEM
AS THEY TRY SINGING OVER ME
I DON'T SEEM TO WEAR THE SAME CLOTHES AS THEM
AS THEY DON'T SEEM TO DRESS LIKE ME
I CERTAINLY DON'T EAT THEIR UNKIND FOOD
THERES NO REASON OR PLACE TO EAT ANIMALS
OR ANY CREATURE WITH A FACE
EVER BY THE HUMAN BEINGS UNKIND RACE

205

EVERYBODY HAS DARK DAYS AND NIGHTS
EVERYBODY HAS GOOD TIMES IN THE PARK
EVERYTHING THAT SHINES
IS NOT NECESSARILY BRIGHT
FOR SOME THINGS ARE BETTER
DONE IN THE DARK

206

WHEN WAS THE LAST TIME YOU EXHALED
LIFE AS FRESH AS THE AIR YOU INHALED
WHEN YOU LET GO
DOES ANYONE OUT THERE REALLY KNOW
LOVE LIFE
LIVING LIKE LOVERS
BEING EACH OTHER
AT THE SAME TIME
DOES ANYONE REALLY MIND LOVE
YOUR A BREATH OF FRESH AIR I INHALED
YOU BRING JOY TO LIFE
EVERY TIME YOU SMILE I CAN'T FAIL
I'M ONLY ABLE TO LOVE YOU
I AM TOTALLY NAILED

207

NiC n Al
R NOT MY PALS
Al n NiC
ARE VERY VERY SiC
DO U KNOW Y
THEY WILL HELP TO
MAKE U DIE

208

ONE EATS TO LIVE
ONE DOES NOT LIVE TO EAT
THERE ARE MILLIONS JUST LIKE ME
HERE AND OVERSEAS
THOSE WHO CHOOSE TO LIVE TO EAT
THEIR OVER WEIGHT BODIES BORDER ON OBESE

209

THEY ARE ACTORS ACTING
NOT BEING THEMSELVES
THEY'RE JUST ACTING
THEY LOVE NOT BEING THEMSELVES
LOVE THEY ARE ACTING
BECAUSE WHEN THEY ARE BEING THEMSELVES
THEY'RE NOT ACTING
BECAUSE WHEN YOU ARE ACTING
YOU CAN BE SOMEONE ELSE

210

IS THERE A MAN OUT THERE
A REAL MAN WITH BALLS
WHO'S NOT AFRAID TO SPEAK OF THIS
WE WILL NOT TOLERATE FASCISTS
IS THERE A MAN OUT HERE
A REAL MAN WITH NO FEAR
WHO DOES NOT WEAR A CAPE
WHO WILL NOT TOLERATE RAPE
WE NEED MEN GENTLEMEN
WHOSE WILL IS TO DEFEND
THE HUMAN RIGHTS OF WOMEN
AND ALL OF OUR CHILDREN
JEREMY CORBYN

211

THEY HAD A DUCK
AT NIGHT
AND A PHEASANT
MORNING

212

WE DO NOT KNOW OF ANY OTHER RELIGION
THAN THE MUSLIM FAITH
THAT STRAPS BOMB JACKETS TO THEMSELVES
TO COMMIT SUICIDE IN THE MIDDLE OF A CROWD
OF OPPOSING BELIEVERS
IN A CONSCIOUS ATTEMPT TO MURDER
AS MANY OF THESE OTHER FAITHS
WHY ARE MUSLIMS IN THE FRONT LINE
OF THE TERRORISTS ACT OF 2005
ONLY MUSLIM FAITH PERSONS
WEAR BOMB JACKETS TO KILL
NOT ONLY THEMSELVES BUT OTHER FAITHS TOO

213

TIME DISAPPEARS
WHEN YOU ARE A BREATH AWAY
TIMELESS AVENUES TO EXPLORE
WITH YOU WHEN TIME STANDS STILL
IT'S JUST OVER THE HILL WHEN
IT'S JUST YOU AND ME DEAR
TIME DISAPPEARS

214

I WAS BOOTED AND SUITED
ON MY WAY TO THE MORGUE
I HAD TO IDENTIFY
MY MOTHER MAUDE
SHE HAD BEEN ILL BEFORE
BUT NOT AS BAD AS THEY SAY
TILL I GOT THE CALL
SHE HAD PASSED AWAY
MY MOTHER MAUDE
I LEFT IN THE MORGUE
I LEFT WITH MY MOTHER MAUDES
MONO GENETIC INHERITANCE
ONE OF MORE THAN 6000

215

WHEN DOES A GAMBLER
BECOME A RISK TAKER
WHEN DOES A RISK TAKER
BECOME RESPECTABLE
WHEN ONE WEARS A SUIT
PLAYING THE CITY STOCK MARKETS
AND WHEN THE CITY STOCK MARKETS
FALL SO DOES THE RESPECTABLE RISK TAKER
WHOM AFTER ALL IS JUST A GAMBLER

216

FIREWORKS DISPLAY
AN OBSCENE SHOW OF AFFLUENCE
WEALTH WASTED WHERE WATERS WEEP
THE SAD TEARS OF ON LOOKERS ASKING
IS THIS ALL YOU COULD COME UP WITH
IS THIS THE BEST YOU COULD DO
CELEBRATING LIFE IN THE 21s CENTURY
COLOURFUL RAINBOWS
GONE IN A BANG
AS THE DUBAI HOTEL OPENED
KYLIE SANG

217

WAITING ON THE BACK PORCH
THE SUN GOING DOWN
IT'S A BEAUTIFUL SIGHT
WITH THE MOON COMING ROUND
I'M LOOKING OUT FOR YOU
I'M LOOKING TOO FOR STARS
AND THERE YOU WERE
I HEARD THE DOGS BARK
AS YOU WALKED OUT OF THE DARK
YOU LIT UP LIKE A STAR

218

LIFE ON THE BREAD LINE
AIN'T SO PRETTY
YOU DREAM OF GETTING OUT
STILL LOOKING PRETTY
LIFE CAN BE GOOD
FAIR OR SAD MAYBE
BUT YOU WILL PROBABLY
EXPERIENCE ALL THREE

219

I'VE SPENT CHRISTMAS
ON AN OCEAN
I'VE SPENT CHRISTMAS
BY THE SEA
I'VE SPENT CHRISTMAS
IN AN AIRCRAFT
I'VE SPENT CHRISTMAS
ON SKIES
I'VE SPENT CHRISTMAS
UP A MOUNTAIN
I'VE SPENT CHRISTMAS
WITH FROZEN PEAS
ON MY KNEE CAPS
BESIDE SNOW CAPPED MOUNTAINS
BECAUSE I CAN'T SKI

220

YOU MUST BE ON THE WRONG DRUGS
IF YOU HIT SOMEONE AND THEN THROW UP
YOU MUST BE ON THE WRONG DRUGS
IF YOU KEEP FALLING DOWN AND YOU CAN'T STAND UP
YOU MUST BE ON THE WRONG DRUGS
SITTING IN A CELL AND YOUR BANGED UP
YOU MUST BE ON THE WRONG DRUGS
IF YOUR IN AN AMBULANCE SOMETHINGS UP
YOU MUST BE ON THE WRONG DRUGS
IF YOUR TOLD IN HOSPITAL YOUR LIVERS UP
YOU MUST BE ON THE WRONG DRUGS

221

TRiUMPh IS RIGHT
BRAZILS NEW PRESIDENT
JAIR BOLSONARO STATES
LET THE PEOPLE BARE ARMS
SELL THEM GUNS AND HOPE
THERE AGAIN HE IS BACKED
BY THE USA AND THE POPE

222

NEVER BEFORE HAVE I STOOD
IN FRONT OF SO MANY
PLAYING MY MUSIC
FOR THE AWARENESS OF
HUNTINGTONS DISEASE
ON A PLINTH IN TRAFALGAR SQUARE
ON THE 12th SEPT 2009 at 10pm
WITH MY DEAR FRIEND ROBIN bee-gee BENEATH
TRYING TO PUT ME OFF
WAVING & SHOUTING KEVIN KEVIN
I EMBODIED ALL THOSE
WHO SHOULD HAVE BEEN STANDING THERE
ON THE 3rd VACANT PLINTH IN TRAFALGAR SQUARE
WHERE I & 2399 OTHERS BECAME
PLINTHIANS FOR ONE HOUR

223

LORDS 1934
THE YOUNG HAVE NOT EXPERIENCED BEING OLD
WHERE AS THE OLD HAVE EXPERIENCED BEING YOUNG
WISDOM COMES NOT WHEN YOUR YOUNG
WISDOM COMES ONLY WHEN YOUR OLD
IRONICALLY MIDDLE AGE DOES NOT BRING
THE FORESIGHT OF THE FUTURE
IN THEIR 50s & 60s OLD AGE SEEMS FARAWAY
WHY ARE OUR NURSING HOMES
NOT FIT FOR PURPOSE
NO ONE BELIEVES
THEY WILL EVER END UP IN ONE
ONE SUPPOSES

224

IF YOU MARRY A MAN IN A SUIT
HE IS UNLIKELY TO UNBLOCK A SINK
EMPTY THE DISHWASHER HOOVER OR COOK
WHY BECAUSE HE WEARS A BLOODY SUIT
WITH ANOTHER MAN WEARING HIS JEANS
HES READY TO COOK HOOVER AND CLEAN
WITH THE SINK UNBLOCKED AND
THE HEDGES ALL CHOPPED
I HEAR YOU SAY
JEAN THERAPY
WORKS FOR ME

225

SOUND BITE MASSACRE
BULLET SHOT VERBAL ABUSE

226

THIS HOUSE HAS BEEN LOVED
AND IS VERY PEACEFUL
WITH MANY WORDS SPOKEN
IN LOVE NOT EVIL
THE HOUSE OWES US NOTHING
WE OWE ALL TO IT
APPRECIATE THE CONTENTS
AND BE CONTENT LIVING WITHIN IT

227

ONE CAN IMAGINE GOING BLIND
ON THE OTHER HAND ONE CAN'T
IT'S TOO DEVASTATINGLY DEFINED
YOUR BLIND SO STAND UP TURN ROUND
FIND THE REMOTE TURN THE SOUND DOWN

228

I KNEW PERSEVERANCE
HE WAS A PERSISTENT CHAP
INVARIABLY HE KEEPS AT YOU
UNTIL HE NEEDS A NAP
AL COHOL IS THE SAME
WHEN HE GETS DOWN YOUR THROAT
THE PROCESS ONE LOVES TO REPEAT
AS YOU RETCH AGAIN YOU BLOAT
NIC OTINE MAY TAKE TOP DOG
IF YOU COUNT DYING FOR A SMOKE
TOBACCO PRODUCTS SOLD EVERYWHERE
BUT YOU CAN'T SMOKE THEM HERE
THERE OR ANYWHERE
AS FOR DIC TATORIAL
HE TENDED TO DICTATE
HIS TYRANNICAL CHARACTERISTICS
A VERY OVER BEARING HOUSE MATE

229

THERES NO FUTURE IN THE PAST
AND NO TIME LIKE THE PRESENT
THE FUTURE DEPENDS
ON WHAT WE DO PRESENTLY
SO CATCH A DREAM
WONDER WITH A STAR
THINK OF ANOTHER WAR
HOWS IT GOING SO FAR

230

THERE IS NO SUCH THING AS MEAT
JUST A WORD THAT RHYMES WITH EAT
WHAT YOU EAT IS ANIMAL FLESH
IF ITS CHICKEN
LEG WING OR BREAST
HAMBURGERS ARE
PIGS COWS AND BULLS
CARNIVORES EAT TILL YOUR FULL
5 POUNDS OF ROTTING FLESH
SHALL BE IN YOUR GUT
BY THE TIME YOU ARE 50
ITS NOT CANCEROUS OR IS IT BUT
THERE IS NO SUCH THING AS MEAT
JUST A WORD THAT RHYMES WITH EAT
SCIENTIST WERE CHALLENGED
WITH A MILLION POUND PRIZE
TO DEVELOP LIVING FLESH TO EAT
AN APPROPRIATE NAME COMES TO MIND
MEAT

231

DON'T JUDGE ME
I DON'T NEED
NO INVISIBLE LIFE SUPPORT
LIKE YOU SEE
I DON'T NEED YOU
TO JUDGE ME
BECAUSE I WON'T BUDGE
TILL YOU CAN SEE
THERES ONLY THIS LIFE
WITH NO SUPPORT GROUP
ONLY LOVE

232

RELIGIOUS INDOCTRINATIONS OF CRUELTY
TO ANIMALS AND HUMANS IS ACCEPTABLE
IN THEIR BELIEFS
RELIGIONS AND EVERYTHING THEY STAND FOR
DO NOT STOP WARS
ON THE CONTRARY
RELIGIONS CAUSE WARS

233

INDIVIDUALLY
YOU GET RIDICULED
FOR SAYING IT HOW IT IS
YOU GET PICKED ON FOR SAYING
THERES TOO MUCH SEX OR VIOLENCE IT'S OBSCENE
YET IT'S ON OUR SCREENS
IT'S IN MAGAZINES YOU KNOW WHAT WE MEAN
IT'S PRINTED AND PUBLISHED
ON BILL BOARDS AND POSTER BOARDS
DIGITISED AND COMPUTERISED THERE FOR ALL
TO DOWNLOAD AND PRINT OR EVEN CALL
YET TO SPEAK OF IT WOW
FOR SAYING IT HOW IT IS
YOU GET RIDICULED
FOR BEING AN INDIVIDUAL

234

ARTISTS MAKE THEM
ATHLETES BREAK THEM
RECORDS ARE MADE TO PLAY
OR BE BROKEN
LISTEN TO THEM SPIN
WATCH THEM AS THEY WIN
LOSE OR BREAK
CHANGE THE RECORD
IT'S NOT TOO LATE

235

DIGITAL CITIZENS
WE HAVE BECOME
SPEAKING ON DIGITAL
APPARATUSES TO SOMEONE
ON WIRELESS COMPUTERS
AND MOBILE PHONES
THE DIGITAL CITIZEN
IS NEVER ALONE

236

THERE ARE THOSE OF YOU
WHO CONFESS THEIR DEEDS
THE GOOD ONES AND THE BAD IT SEEMS
THERE IS SOMEONE LOOKING OVER
YOUR ALTERED MIND
IS YOUR RELIEF COUNTING BEADS HUMBLY
IN A SELF HYPNOTIC STATE OF BELIEF
THERE IS A BETTER LIFE
WHEN YOU ARE DEAD
WHO PUTS THIS INSIDE ONES HEAD
CIVILISATIONS
PAST AND PRESENT
USE THE MIND TO RULE THE PEASANT
CONTRARY TO THE BELIEF OF ALL
WE'RE NOT GOING TO BANG
OUR HEADS AGAINST WALLS

237

RESPECT
SINCERELY I APOLOGISE
MY FEELINGS
THEY HAVE BEEN COMPROMISED
AS I FOUND TO MY SURPRISE
I'D BEEN STARING AT YOU
AS YOU WALKED BY
I HAVE NEVER FELT LIKE THIS BEFORE
SPEECHLESS DUMB WITH AN OPEN JAW
MY FEET WERE FIXED AS I ADORED
THIS WOMAN I'D NEVER SEEN BEFORE
YOUR HAIR YOUR CLOTHES
YOUR STYLE YOUR MOOD
YOUR PERFUME SMELT EXOTIC TOO
I WAS CLOSE ENOUGH TO BREATHE IN YOU
IF ONLY IT WAS TO BE TRUE
BUT I TRUSTED MYSELF
NEVER TO TROUBLE YOU

238

MY NAME IS DICK
AND IT SUITS MY PERSONALITY
I AM THICK
IN FEMALES COMPANY
I DON'T SEEM TO FIT
IN THEIR REALITY
I SWEAR I SHIT MYSELF
WHEN THEY'RE AROUND ME
I NEVER KNOW WHAT TO SAY
WHEN WORDS GET IN THE WAY

239

ALL RELIGIONS COULD FEED THE WORLD
WHY DO THEY CHOOSE NOT TO

240

ALL THAT I HAVE SEEN
WITH ALL I NOW KNOW
WITH MY EYES WIDE OPEN
PEN DOWN BOOK CLOSED
IF MUSIC BE THE FOOD OF LOVE
I SHALL NOT GO HUNGRY
MY LOVER IS A MINSTREL
WHO FEEDS ME CONSTANTLY

241

TO FRACK OR
NOT TO FRACK
THIS IS THE
FRACTURING QUESTION
NEVER

242

IGNORANCE IS BLISS
WEARING A BOMB VEST THAT FITS
BELIEVING YOUR RIGHT
YET YOU CANNOT READ NOR WRITE
FAITH IN ONES PEERS
TRUSTING YOUR SUPERIORS
THEY READ FROM A BOOK
THAT TELLS YOU TO FIGHT
YOU DON'T KNOW WHAT TO DO
YOU HAVE NO LIFE
SO YOUR OFFERED ANOTHER ONE
DOES THE VEST FIT ALRIGHT

243

POPE FRANCIS IS THE HEAD OF THE CATHOLIC CHURCH
CULPABLE FOR HIS CARDINALS BISHOPS & PRIESTS
THE POPE THEREFORE SHOULD BE CASTRATED
ALONG WITH HIS GANG OF PAEDOPHILE RAPISTS
THE POPE CAN RESOLVE THIS TODAY FOREVER
IF HE ONLY READ HIS FLAT BIBLE BOOK
AND TURN ALL HIS MALE DISCIPLES
INTO CASTRATED BLOODY EUNUCHS

244

RUGBY NEVER APPEALED TO ME
I'D HAVE TO FATTEN UP AND BE MUSCULARLY
FOOTBALL I COULD BE ATHLETIC THATS FINE
AND YOU GET 5 MORE MINUTES AT HALF TIME
BUT CRICKET YOU GET DINNER
AND AT 4pm YOU GET TEA
GUESS WHICH ONE APPEALED TO ME

245

GOT MY FINGER IN MY POCKET
IT TAKES A LOT TO GET IT OUT
IT NEEDS A MESSAGE THAT IS POSITIVE
A TECHNO PROBLEM TO THINK ABOUT
AN INSPIRATIONAL THEORY OR
A CREATIONAL STUDY WORK OUT
THERES A MESSAGE ON THE PHONE
IT READS MUM
I'D BETTER GET IT OUT

246

OPEN YOUR EYES
YOU WON'T SEE A SMILE
YOU WON'T HEAR A THANK YOU
PARDONS ARE DISMISSED
PARDONS DON'T EXIST
WITH BATHROOMS TO VISIT
AND TOILETS TO EXIT
THE TOAST YOU GRAB IT
ON THE BUS YOU'LL EAT IT
IT'S THE LITTLE THINGS
THAT GET YOU THROUGH
AND THIS MORNING
IT WAS TOAST

247

WE'RE NOT BORN
WITH RELIGIOUS VIEWS
WE'RE NOT BORN
A POLITICAL WAY
WE'RE NOT ALL BORN STRAIGHT
SOME OF US ARE BORN GAY
BUT IN THE LOTTERY OF LIFE
MOST WON'T MAKE A DAY
ONE COUPLE GETS
ONE CHANCE EVERY 4 WEEKS
THAT IS JUST
13 TIMES A YEAR
WHEN ONE THINKS OF
ALL THE PEOPLE ALIVE
THATS OVER 7 BILLIONS
MAKES ONE THINK OF
THE BILLIONS
THAT ARE NOT BORN
EVERY YEAR

248

LIFE IS BUT A DREAM
FOR YOU
A DAY IS ANOTHER SCENE
FOR YOU
THE WORLD IS JUST A STAGE
FOR YOU
TO PLAY ALL THE PARTS
FOR YOU ARE THE STAR

249

IT'S A SICK WORLD
WHERE RELIGIOUS DRIVEN INDOCTRINATIONS
SEPARATES AND DIVIDES
PEOPLES FROM PEOPLES
TEARS ARE SHED BLOOD IS SPILT
SILENCE AND SECRECY
BUILDS WALLS OF HATRED
ALL THIS IN THE NAME OF A GOD
ALLAH JESUS & MOSES
THE LEADERS OF THESE THREE
ARCHAIC RELIGIONS
OUGHT TO BE ASHAMED OF THEMSELVES
AND SHAMED BY THE REST OF THE WORLD

250

IF YOU ARE UP AND RUNNING
THIS ONE IS FOR YOU
THE HOUR OF BLUE
BEFORE SUN AND AFTER MOON
THE CLEAR OPAQUE HUE
TRANSCENDS UP AND THROUGH
LIKE A MIST LIKE THE DEW
THE COLOURS OF AZURE
PALE AND FADE LIKE STEAM
LIKE A STREAM
EBBS AND FLOWS
BLUE BLOOMS OF SNOW
DRIFTING ON A TIDE
TO WHEREVER ONE KNOWS
STILL LIKE A SEA
ONES EYES PERCEIVE
THE LIGHT BLUE LIGHT
AS ONE LOOKS UP TO SEIZE
THE LAST BLUE HUES OF
THE HOUR OF BLUE

251

DISTILLED DRINKS
BREWERY BEER DRINKERS
FERMENTING FRUITS FROM
VINTAGE VINES
RED WHITE OR ROSE
SPARKLING OR CHAMPAGNE WINES
THESE ALCOHOLIC DRINKS ARE A STIMULANT
LEAVING ONE AND ALL DRUNK & DISTANT

252

PHARMACEUTICAL
DRUG DEALERS TO THE HUMAN POPULATION
FARMERCEUTICALS
DEAL PESTICIDES HERBICIDES INSECTICIDES
POISONOUS AND TOXIC CHEMICALS ON THE LAND
AND ALL THE ANIMAL POPULATION
NEARLY HALF THE WORLDS ANTIBIOTICS
FED TO LIVESTOCK BECAUSE
DISEASE IS IN THE CARNIVORES FOOD CHAIN
NEEDLESS TORTUROUS FOOD FOR BIGOTS

253

ONE BELIEVES ONE IS RIGHT
TO FEATHER ONES OWN NEST
FURTHER ONES OWN INTERESTS
AND CARVE OUT ONES OWN DREAMS
WHATEVER THE MEANS
THE MODERATE CONSERVATIVE OUTLOOK
IT SEEMS AUSTERITY WORKS
FOR THE PRIVILEGED ONE THOUSAND
THEY WERE WORTH £250 BILLIONS BEFORE
NOW THEY ARE WORTH £750 BILLIONS
NOT BAD FOR SITTING ON ONES HANDS
IF THEY ALL PAID THEIR TAX
EVERYBODY WOULD BE HOUSED FED AND EDUCATED
WITH A SOCIAL CARE SOCIETY SECOND TO NONE
AND THEY WOULD NOT NEED THE PARANOID SECURITY
THEY LIVE BEHIND THEIR OWN MAKING OF AUSTERITY
FEAR EXASPERATES FEAR
USED BY KINGS RULERS RELIGIONS

FOR THOUSANDS OF YEARS
TO SUPPRESS THEIR CITIZENS SUBJECTS
THE CIVILIAN POPULATION TO ABIDE BY THEIR LAWS
WITH A FEARFUL SUBMISSIVE SOCIETY OF WORKERS
ONE HAS THE MAN POWER TO MAKE AND MAN MACHINES
TO FIRE ARSENAL AND WEAPONS OF DESTRUCTION AND
BE USED TO MAKE AN ARMY OF FODDER FOR DESTRUCTION
AND LEVEL THE PLAYING FIELDS OF AN ENEMY OR FOE
THEN ENABLING ONES OWN
CIVILIAN CORPORATIONS OF CONSTRUCTION
TO RE BUILD THAT COUNTRY AND
SOCIETY ON ONES OWN TERMS

254

WHEN CLIMBERS ARE CHALLENGED
OF THEIR SELFISH ACTIVITY
THEIR USUAL REPLY IS
COMPARATIVE TO ROAD TRAFFIC ACCIDENTS
PARAMEDICS DO NOT PUT THEIR LIVES AT RISK
EVERY TIME LIKE Mt RESCUE TEAMS
FLYING IN HELICOPTERS
WITH FREEZING CONDITIONS
PUTTING THE TEAMS THE MEDICS
THE CREWS AND HELICOPTERS AT RISK
LOOKING BEYOND THE COST OF
HELICOPTERS AND FUEL
IS THE HUMAN COST OF LIVES
ALL SEARCHING FOR YOU
THE ONES WHO LOVE THE THRILL OF
DICING WITH DEATH
JUST DON'T EXPECT ANY SYMPATHY
OR RESPECT
A TOTAL WASTE OF ENERGY

255

YOU TALK THE TALK
IN SHOES YOU BOUGHT
TO WALK THE WALK
IN SHOES YOU LIKE
FROM A RAINBOW OF COLOURS
COMFORTABLE AND LIGHT
THEY COME WITH A TICK
YOU KNOW THEY ARE NIKE

256

ONE CAN TALK FOR HOURS
ABOUT THIS ONE WORD
THAT IS SO SMALL IN ITSELF
YET HAS THE MOST PROFOUND
DEEP AND MEANINGFUL EMOTIONS
KNOWN TO MANKIND
WITH EVERY HUMAN LONGING
TO BECOME IT
DESIRE IT EVEN PRAY FOR IT
WISH AND SEND IT OR
ONE COULD ABUSE IT
THROW IT BACK IN THEIR FACE
TREAT IT WITH CONTEMPT YES
YOU CAN HURT PEOPLE WITH THIS WORD
THIS WORD CAN MAKE ONE GRIEVE
EVEN TO DEATH OVER THIS
LITTLE WORD OR
LIVE THE MOST PURE
HAPPY LIFE FOR ONESELF
CONSCIOUS OF THIS WORD
WHICH HAS BROUGHT US ALL HERE
LOVE

257

CAN ONE
BEG A DOG TO TEACH
DANCE A BEAR TO BEAT
EAT A COW TO SLAUGHTER
THEN PUT ITS SKIN ON YOUR FEET

258

IF THERES NO HEAVEN
IF THERES NO HELL
IF THERES NO GOD
IF THERES NO DEVIL
IF THERES NO RELIGION
IF THERES NO BELIEF
IF THERES NO FEAR
ONE CAN LIVE
FREEDOM

259

MEDITATION
SELF HYPNOTIC STATE OF BELIEF

260

ONE IS A DRUG TAKER
ONE IS NOT AN ADDICT
ONE DOES NOT NECESSARILY GO AROUND
CRAVING FOR A HIT
ONE HAS ILLNESSES AND DISEASE
AND PROBLEMS LIKE YOU
ONE TAKES PRESCRIPTION DRUGS
AND RECREATIONAL TOO
ONE HATES ALCOHOL
ONE HATES NICOTINE
ONE HATES THE INSTITUTIONS
THAT RELY ON THEIR MEANS
ONE HAS TO TAKE OFFENCE
WHEN ONES CALLED AN ADDICT
BY DEATH TOBACCO SMOKERS AND
DYING DRINKING ALCOHOLICS

261

TO BE OR NOT TO BE
A CARNIVORE OR VEGAN
ONE DOES NOT NEED TO HUNT NOR GATHER
THERE ARE ORGANIC FAIR TRADERS
HEALTH SHOPS AND SUPERMARKETS
SO ONE CAN BE A VEGAN
OR A BIGOT THAT EATS CRUELTY & FEAR
WITH NO DISCIPLINE ONE STAMPS ONES' FEET
ONE WON'T CHANGE ONES' CRAVINGS
YES IT'S ONLY THE TASTE AND TEXTURE
THE TASTE OF WHAT ONE EATS

262

IMAGINE A SOCK
ON THE OUTSIDE OF A SHOE
IMAGINE BEING THE SHOE
HAVING THE LIFE SQUEEZED OUT OF YOU
IMAGINE THE SHOCK
AND THE UNCOMFORTABLE TRUTH
THAT IF THE TABLES WERE TURNED
WOULD YOU ACCEPT LIFE
BEING SQUEEZED OUT OF YOU
IMAGINE YOU ARE UNDERWEAR
ON THE OUTSIDE OF YOUR CLOTHES
IMAGINE THE UNDERWEAR
BEING EXPOSED
IMAGINE THE SHOCK
FOR EVERYONE YOU SUPPOSE
JUST IMAGINE IF YOU WERE
THE UNDERWEAR EXPOSED
IMAGINE YOURSELF WRONG
AND BEING CORRECTED
IMAGINE YOURSELF BOOKED
AND BEING SUSPENDED
IMAGINE YOURSELF HOOKED
AND BEING AN ADDICT
IMAGINE YOURSELF DEAD
AND BEING CREMATED

263

COMING HERE I NOTICED
AN OLD MAN ON THE STREET
HE HAD HOLES IN HIS SHOES
AND PROBABLY HOLES IN HIS FEET
HIS RAINCOAT AND TROUSERS
WERE TORN TO SHREDS
ALONG WITH HIS JUMPER
AND WHAT WAS LEFT ON HIS HEAD
HE LOOKED AT ME
AS I BUMPED INTO HIM
HIS EYES SET DEEP
SUNKEN WITH GIN
HE GRABBED MY ARM
AND SPUN ME AROUND
I HAD TO LAUGH
AS HE HAD TO FROWN

GIVE ME A BREAK
OR SOME MONEY INSTEAD
YOU CAN SEE I'M BROKE
AND I NEED A BED

MORE LIKE A SMOKE AND
A DRINK FOR YOUR HEAD
I BET HE WON'T GO
TO THE HOSTEL OVER THERE
IT'S TIME HE FED HIS SPIRIT
NOT A SPIRIT TO FEED HIM
SO I ASKED HIM
WHAT HE DID
AND HE REPLIED WITH A GRIN

QUANTUM PHYSICS
IT FUCKED ME AND MANKIND
NOW I DRINK GIN
IT'S LEGAL AND CHEAP

THEN HE LEFT WITH MY FIVER
A WINK AND A GRIN

264

I WON'T DRINK WITH AL

I WON'T SMOKE WITH NIC

I WON'T CHASE DRAGONS

I WON'T BECOME OBESE

I WON'T EAT THE FLESH

I WON'T WEAR THE SKIN

OF ANY CREATURE WITH A FACE

IT DISGUSTS ME IT'S A DISGRACE

I AM A VEGAN

265

THEY STILL KILL ELEPHANTS YOU KNOW

THEY BLAME IT ON THE POACHERS AND SO

THE TROPHY HUNTERS ALL HAVE LICENSES TO SHOW

AND SIGNED OFF BY THE BRITISH GOVERNMENTS MICHAEL GOVE

266

WHEN ONES HAPPY
ONES BEING SELFISH
ONES NOT THINKING
OF ONES MOTHERS
OF ONES BROTHER
ONES ONLY THINKING
OF ONE OTHER
AND HOW LONG CAN ONE
STAY BLIND FOR
BEFORE ONE REALISES THIS
ONES BEING SELFISH
UNLESS YOUR WISE
AND YOU COMPROMISE
TO BE HAPPY IN BLISS
SOMETIMES
YOU HAVE TO BE SELFISH
SOMETIMES

267

ONE THANKS THE SOLDIERS
ONE THANKS THE PILOTS
ONE THANKS THE NAVY
AND ALL PERSONNEL
WHO DIED FOR US
ONE THANKS THEM ALL
FOR THEIR COURAGE
AND THEIR COMMITMENTS
IN THEIR BELIEFS
THAT WE SHALL BE FREE
ONE CHERISHES THE LIFE
AND THE VOTE
AND THE FREEDOM
THEY HAVE LEFT US ALL
MAY YOU ALL NOW
REST IN PEACE
MAKE LOVE NOT WARS
OPEN MINDS OPEN DOORS
OPEN HEARTS OVER JOY
FOR EVERY GIRL AND EVERY BOY
MAKE DREAMS COME TRUE
FOR ME FOR YOU
FOR ALL FOR EVERYONE
TO ENJOY THROUGH AND THROUGH
HOW MUCH IS IN THE PEACE CHEST
THE WAR CHEST IS OVERFLOWING
HOW MUCH IS IN THE PEACE CHEST
PLEASE KEEP THE PEACE CHEST
OVERFLOWING
VOTE SOLIDARITY FOR
A SOCIAL DAWNING
JEREMY CORBYNS
GOING TO COME CALLING

268

LOVE BEFORE LIFE

LIFE BEFORE LOVE

DO YOU LIVE TO LOVE

OR DO YOU LOVE TO LIVE

LIFE OF LOVE

LOVE OF LIFE

IT'S ONLY A DILEMMA

IF YOU COMPROMISE

YOUR LOVE LIFE

IT'S ALL WATER UNDER THE BRIDGE

IF YOU ARE IN LOVE

269

IF OR WHEN YOU FEEL INTIMIDATED

JUST REMEMBER THIS

WE'RE ALL HUMAN BEINGS

IMAGINE THEM TAKING A PISS

270

I'M INTO I.T.
I'M INTO THE NET
I'M INTERACTIVE
WITH THE REST OF THE SET
BUT JUST SITTING THERE
LEAVING WORDS IN THE AIR
YOU ARE NOT MEETING PEOPLE
WHO ARE WAITING OUT THERE
TO SING WITH AND LAUGH WITH
AND TO HAVE A GOOD DANCE
AND FIND SOME HAPPINESS
INSTEAD OF SITTING IN A TRANCE
I'M INTO I.T.
THE I.T. SHIT
BUT GET INTERACTIVE
WITH PEOPLE ON THE STREET
CAUSE THATS WHERE TO MEET
IT'S COOL AND IT'S SWEET
SO BRING YOUR LAPPY WITH YOU
DOWNLOAD AND COME WITH IT

271

GONE ARE THE DAYS
WE COULD PICK KIDS UP
IN OUR ARMS
GONE ARE THE DAYS
WE COULD SMOTHER THEM
WITH CHARMS
GONE ARE THE DAYS
WE COULD
KISS A CHILD
ALL DOWN TO THE ACTIONS
OF VILE PAEDOPHILES
CHILDHOOD INNOCENCE
CHALLENGED ONCE MORE
NOT JUST BY THE TELLY
OR THE UNCLOSED DOOR
NOR BY THEIR CLASSMATES
AND WHAT THEY SAY
BUT BY VILE PAEDOPHILES
ON THE INTERNET HIGHWAY
GONE ARE THE DAYS
WE COULD SMILE
AT A CHILD
GONE ARE THE DAYS
WE COULD BEFRIEND
A CHILD
GONE ARE THE DAYS
TO EVEN HELP
A CHILD
ALL DOWN TO THE ACTIONS
OF VILE PAEDOPHILES
CHILDHOOD INNOCENCE
PROTECT THEM MORE
ALL PARENTS WISH THEM
TO BE CHILDREN FOR SURE
BUT SOME VILE ADULTS

WISH TO DEFILE
THE MINDS OF OUR CHILDREN
THEY'RE CALLED VILE PAEDOPHILES
GONE ARE THE DAYS
WE COULD GIVE
CHILDREN SWEETS
GONE ARE THE DAYS
WE COULD SAY
HI IN THE STREET
GONE ARE THE DAYS
WE COULD HUG
A CHILD
ALL DOWN TO THE ACTIONS
OF THOSE VILE PAEDOPHILES

272

DON'T GIVE UP
LOVE IT'S WORTH LIVING FOR
DON'T GIVE UP
PEACE IT'S SO BEAUTIFUL
DON'T GIVE UP
LIFE IT'S WORTH LIVING FOR
DON'T GIVE UP
RESPECT YOUR SELF A LOT MORE
DON'T GIVE UP
YOUR MORALS ARE WHAT YOU STAND FOR
DON'T GIVE UP
YOUR PHILOSOPHY LIFE'S WORTH LIVING FOR
DON'T GIVE UP
YOUR HUMAN RIGHTS OUR FREEDOM AND LIBERTY
DON'T GIVE UP
YOUR VOTE PEOPLE HAVE DIED FOR
DON'T GIVE UP
ON YOURSELF YOU ARE BEAUTIFUL
DON'T GIVE UP LOVE
DON'T GIVE UP LIFE
TILL THE END MY FRIEND

273

AS THE WAVES CARESS
THE SANDS ON THE SHORE
THE BREEZE FLUTTERS
THE LEAVES OF THE BEECH
MY HAND COMBS
THE LENGTH OF YOUR HAIR
AS OUR EYES EMBRACE
OUR PASSIONATE STARE
WITH FORCES KNOWN
BEYOND OUR TIME
WHICH MAKES A MAN
AND A WOMAN ENTWINE
THE POWER OF KNOWLEDGE
AND LOVE AND LUST
SHALL FOREVER BE LIVED
IN THE LIVES OF US

274

I AM A FOX
I'M GIVEN THE RUN AROUND
BY HUNTERS ON HORSES
WITH PACKS OF HOUNDS
THEY CALL IT SPORTING
CHASING AFTER ME
TIL THEY RUN ME TO GROUND
TO BE RIPPED UP BY HOUNDS
THEY CALL IT SPORTING
EXHAUSTING ME
WITH PACKS OF HOUNDS
PLEASE JUST LET ME BE

275

ON THOSE DARKEST DAYS OF WINTER
WHEN THE COLD WINDS BLOW TO GALES
REMEMBER DAFFODILS APPEAR IN SPRING
FROM BENEATH THE WHITE FALLS OF SNOW

276

BE KIND BE HONEST
BE POLITE AND FAIR
SPEAK THE TRUTH
SPEAK YOUR MIND
SPEAK TO ALL WHO CARE
LISTEN TO THE FAINTEST
LOOK AFTER THE WEAK
AND LOOK OUT FOR THE BULLY BOY
OUT THERE ON THE STREET
PLAN FOR TOMORROW ON
THE MERITS OF YESTERDAY
BE SURE TO REMEMBER
TO LIVE FOR TODAY
WITH LOVE IN YOUR HEARTS
AS WITH THE BLOOD IN YOUR VEINS
THE SEEDS THAT YOU SOW
SHALL FOREVER REMAIN
SO SOW THEM WITH PEACE
IN THE MIND OF A CHILD
MAY THEIR INNOCENCE GROW
IN THEIR HEARTS JUST FOR AWHILE
LONGER

277

STOP

EATING

EWE PIG COW

278

HOW MANY SPECIES DOES ONE THINK
MAN HAS NOT DISCOVERED
BUT HAVE MADE EXTINCT

279

THEY TOOK TO THE STREETS
AND THEY MARCHED TO THE SQUARE
WHERE ALL OF THE PEOPLE
WERE PROTESTING THERE
THEY WAVED THEIR BANNERS
AND FLAGS IN THE AIR
ALL DEMANDING TO BE FREE
LIKE YOU AND ME
DANCING WITH BULLETS
LAUGHING WITH SCREAMS
SIRENS OF SILENCE
DROWNING THE DREAMS
OF PEOPLES TURNING
THEIR LIVES TO BE FREE
AS FREE AS THE AIR
THAT WE ALL BREATHE

280

YOU DON'T ALWAYS GET WHAT YOU WANT
YOU DON'T ALWAYS GET WHAT YOU NEED
YOU WON'T ALWAYS GET WHAT YOU NEED
OR WHAT YOU WANT
IT'S WHAT WE GET
WHEN WE LEAST EXPECT
WITH NO REGRETS
IT'S NOT WHAT YOU GET
IT'S WHAT YOU RECEIVE
FROM SOMEONE GIVING
MORE THAN WHATS PERCEIVED
SO WHEN YOUR RECEIVING
SIMPLY BE PLEASING
AND ACCEPT THE GIFT WITH LOVE
WITH NO REASON

281

HOMO SAPIEN   HUMAN BEING   MANKIND
WHEN IN HISTORY HAS HOMO SAPIEN HUMANS BEEN KIND

282

AS AN ADVANCED BREED OF MONKEY
WE ARE THE FIFTH APE NO DOUBT
WE ARE IMPERFECTION
WE GASTRONOMICALLY EXIST
WE QUESTION AND DEMAND ANSWERS
BUT SADLY WE ARE PREPARED
TO KILL LIE SHOUT AND CONQUER TO SURVIVE

283

WHAT IS A WEEKEND
A 19th CENTURY LADY ONCE REMARKED
THE LAST TWO DAYS OF THE WEEK
SATURDAY AND SUNDAYS
WALKING IN SPRING
TAKING IN THE BREEZE
WALKING IN THE SUMMER
WALKING WITH EASE
WALKING IN THE AUTUMN
KICKING THOSE LEAVES
WALKING IN THE WINTER
WELLIES UP TO YOUR KNEES
HOODS UP YOU KNOW
CAN'T GET ENOUGH SNOW
THE WHITE STUFF IS FALLING
YO HO HO WE'RE WALKING IN SNOW
SO WHAT IS A FORTNIGHT
THAT'S FROM ROMAN TIMES
FORT DUTY LASTED 14 DAYS
2 WEEKS ONE BELIEVES FROM SUNDAYS

284

CARNIVORES VEGETARIANS & VEGANS
CAN ALL EAT IN A JEWISH RESTAURANT
ANIMALS FISH FOWL & VEGETABLES KEPT SEPARATE
ALONG WITH ALL UTENSILS THERE'S NO CROSS CONTAMINATE

285

WAS NYE BEVANS N H S BASED UPON THE PRINCIPLE
THAT THE PRIVATE CARPETED ASSET BUILDINGS HOSPITAL PROFITS
FILTER DOWN TO HOUSE THE LINOLEUM NON ASSET PORTACABIN
SPREADS WE NOW HAVE ALL AROUND THE UK
FOR THE NOT SO PRIVATE WORKING CLASS PEOPLE WHO
PAY THEIR NATIONAL INSURANCE EVERY WEEK TO GET
FREE AT RECEPTION HEALTH CARE TESTS AND DIAGNOSTICS
IF SO ONE DOES NOT SEE PORTACABIN SPREADS AROUND
THE PRIVATE HOSPITALS PATRONISED BY PRIVILEGED PATIENTS
WHERE THERE HAS BEEN AN INCREASE IN PRIVATE HEALTH CARE

286

DENIAL DECEIVE PRETEND FALSE FAKE FRAUDULENT
DENY ONESELF THE TRUTH IS LYING
DENIAL OF ONES CANCER
DENIAL OF SELF HARMING
DENIAL OF ALCOHOLISM
DENIAL OF DISEASES LIKE HUNTINGTON'S & ALZHEIMER'S
DENIAL OF ONES EXTRA MARITAL PARTNERSHIP SEX
OR OF ONES CLOSETED SEXUAL ORIENTATIONS
HARMS THE WHOLE DOMINOES RELATIONSHIP SAGA
THAT EVERYONE IN THE VILLAGE NEIGHBOURHOOD
SHALL BE AFFECTED BY

287

IT'S JUST ONE OF THOSE MOMENTS
YOU WISHED YOU HAD A FRIEND
IT'S JUST ONE OF THOSE MOMENTS
YOU WISH YOU COULD COMPREHEND
IT'S JUST ONE OF THOSE SILLY MOMENTS
YOU WISHED YOU HAD A PEN

288

STOP OUR CARBON FOOTPRINT PLEASE
OUR FARMING FOOTPRINT IS FULL OF DISEASE
ONE WONDERS WHAT WOULD CHARLES DARWIN BE
NOT GLAD BUT SAD & MOST ANGRILY DISPLEASED
OBSERVING THE DEVOLUTION OF ALL LIFE IT SEEMS
INCLUDING MAN EARTH AIR AND MARINE

289

LIKE A STREAM FLOWING
IT NEEDS A MOUTH
LIKE AN ALBATROSS FLYING
IT NEEDS A SKY
LIKE A GIANT RED WOOD
IT NEEDS GOOD EARTH
LIKE A NATION DYING
IT NEEDS RE BIRTH

290

MY DAYS WERE STARTED
WITH CHALK AND SLATE
ACHIEVING THE QUILL
AND INKWELL LATE
PIGEONS WE USED
TO COMMUNICATE
TO PEOPLES IN DIFFERENT COUNTRIES
OTHER WORLDS AND STATES
I NOW HOLD A VARIETY
OF GADGETS IN HAND
IT'S A COMPUTER VIDEO CAMERA
TELEPHONE AND SAT NAV
I CAN FIND THE KOGI INDIANS
IN COLOMBIA TO DATE
WHY HAVE THEY NOT FOUND
THE CHALK AND SLATE
A CHALLENGE TO US ALL
WHO LIKE TO COMMUNICATE
THE KOGI INDIANS ARE
TO BE RESPECTED MATES
A PEOPLES WHO HAVE NOT YET
DISCOVERED THE WHEEL
A LONG WAY OFF
DISCOVERING THE QUILL

291

WE COPE WITH MANY THINGS
IN THIS LIFE OF OURS
THE BULLY THE TRICKSTER
THE THIEF AND THE LIAR
THE NOD THE WINK
DO YOU SWIM DO YOU SINK
A SHAKE OF THE HEAD
A FIRM HANDSHAKE INSTEAD
ADRENALINE INTRIGUE
SELF OBSESSIVE ESTEEM
ARROGANT AND JUDGMENTAL
UNTIL YOUR SO FAR UP YOUR ARSE
YOU DO GO MENTAL
ON THE OTHER SIDE OF THINGS
AND LIFE SO IT SEEMS
WE DO COME THROUGH
WITH A NEW VIEW
THAT TODAY IS THE BEST
IT IS BETTER THAN THE REST
FOR THIS MAYBE
THE LAST DAY OF YOUR LIFE
ONE JESTS

292

WHEN CARDINALS ARE VOTING
FOR THEIR NEW POPE
THE BALLOT PAPERS ARE BURNT
AFTER EVERY VOTE
IF THE SMOKE BURNS BLACK
AGAIN THEY MUST VOTE
BUT WHEN THE SMOKES WHITE
IT INFORMS ALL
WE HAVE A NEW POPE

293

I WAKE UP IN THE MORNING
THERE YOU ARE INSIDE MY HEAD
I CAN'T GO TO SLEEP AT NIGHT
WITHOUT YOU IN MY BED
I GET UP AND GO TO WORK
AND THERE YOU ARE AGAIN
TELLING ME YOU LOVE ME
AS I REPEAT THE PHRASE
AND WHEN I GET HOME AT NIGHT
WITH YOU STILL IN MY BRAIN
I READ THE NOTE LEFT ON THE FRIDGE
THANKS BUT GONE TO SPAIN

294

WE'RE KILLING OUR PLANET
WITH TOXIC POLLUTIONS
FIELDS FULL OF ANIMALS
FARTING METHANE GAS AND CO2s TOWARDS MARS
WHERE ONCE NATURAL FORESTS
WERE FILTERING OUT THE AIR
WHERE ONCE NATURAL FORESTS WERE STARS
EACH TIME A FOREST IS LAID BARE
THERE WILL BE NO FILTERING OF AIR
INSTEAD FIELDS OF FARTS
CONDEMNING US FROM THE START
MAN CAN FEED THE WORLD
HE IS MORE THAN ABLE
ONLY IF LIVESTOCK STOPS
AND WE RETURN TO ORGANIC & ARABLE

295

IT'S ONLY A TASTE A TEXTURE
IT'S ONLY BLOOD GUTS AND FLESH
IT'S ONLY A QUESTION A DISCIPLINE TO CHANGE AGAIN
NOT ONLY ONES TASTE BUT ONES CARBON FOOTPRINT OF PAIN

296

THE WORLD IS YOUR OYSTER

FOR THE ALCOHOLIC CARNIVORES

297

OLD AGE BRINGS ON MANY THINGS AND FACTS
ONE OF THESE BEING ONES CATARACTS
ONES OPTOMETRIST WILL ADVISE
PRIVATELY £3000 PER EYE
AND WILL PUT ONE ON THE NHS LIST
FOR CATARACT OPERATION IF ONE PERSISTS
BUT ONE WILL PROBABLY GO BLIND
BEFORE ONES APPOINTMENT ARRIVES

298

AND THERE WILL BE CHILDREN WAVING
IF THEY HAD ARMS
AND THEY WILL BE RUNNING TOO
IF THEY HAD LEGS TO RUN
ALL CLIMBING ON HOPES
AND SLIDING WITH SCREAMS
THROUGH KALEIDOSCOPE MEMORIES
OF NIGHTMARES AND DREAMS
WARS ARE FUTILE WRONG WITH THAT SAID
CHILDREN BARE THE BURDEN AND
THE COST OF THE DEAD

299

THEY WERE THERE ONE MINUTE
THEN GONE THE NEXT
LIKE AN IMPRESSIONISTS DRAWING
THAT DOES NOT EXIST
SHADOWS AND MEMORIES
OF PAST DISTANT DAWNS
REPEATEDLY ETCHED
REMEMBERED AND DRAWN
IF IT WASN'T FOR THE PENCIL / PEN
CAMERA COMPUTER LINK
NO ONE WOULD BELIEVE
WHAT LIFE IS LIKE ON THE BRINK
DON'T BLINK

300

FIRST YOU ARE MY FRIEND
OFFICIALLY MY MATE
SECOND TO NONE MY LOVER
MY ETERNAL SPARRING MATE
YOUR BEAUTY IS OUTWEIGHED
ONLY BY YOUR INTELLECT
AND YOUR CARING CONSCIOUS NATURE
IS COMPLIMENTED WITH A WRY WIT
YOU WERE BLOOMING WHEN I MET YOU
YOU BLOSSOMED IN MOTHERHOOD
AND YOU STILL LOOK BLOOMING ALRIGHT TO ME
YOU CAN STILL PUT ME IN THE MOOD
LASTLY BUT JUST FOR ONE THING
I THOUGHT OF THE OTHER DAY
THE HAND OF LOVE IS HELD OUT TO YOU AND ME
EVERY SINGLE DAY LOVE

301

ONE CAN NEVER FESTER
ONES GOT TO JESTA
KEEP ON YOUR VESTA
ONE IS AN INVESTA
COOL AS A CUCUMBER
ONE MUST NEVER SUCCUMA
KEEP A COOL HEAD UNDER
FROM ATTACKS ASUNDER
BE MINDFUL OF ALL FOLLY
KEEP A HOLD OF YOUR TROLLY
WHEN IT RAINS USE A BROLLY
IF YOU DON'T YOUR A WALLY
IN TIMES OF GRIEF AND STRIFE
USE YOUR HEAD WITH YOUR HEART NOT A KNIFE
IT MAY JUST SAVE A LIFE

WITH NO HEAD IN HANDS STILL ALIVE
FEEL NO PAIN NOTHING NO SORROW
FEEL THE WARMTH THE SMILES BENEATH
THE FACADES BROKEN AND WEAK
AS THE LOVE SMILES BACK ON YOUR CHEEKS
THERES NO SHAME NO WEAKNESS IN THIS
TO SHOW LOVE COMPASSION AND KISS
THE FOE THE ENEMY THE TWIST
YOUR NOT A MAN IF YOU USE YOUR FIST
FEEL NO PAIN NOTHING TOMORROW
FEEL THE LOVE THAT GROWS NO SORROW
FEEL THE LOVE IN THIS
THEN GIVE US A KISS
WHAT IS THE TWIST
GIVE ME A CALL A TEXT A TWITTER
GET IN TOUCH I'M OUT WITH MY SISTER
KEEP IN TOUCH I'M OUT TO LUNCH
KEEP ME IN THE LOOP THEY'RE SERVING SOUP
WATCH OUT WAKE UP WE HAVE TO FACE
THIS WORLD IS FULL OF OUR PLASTIC WASTE
WHERES THE RUBBER FROM YOUR TYRES MATE
WE BREATHE IN SHIT AND WHAT'S ON YOUR PLATE
WATCH OUT WAKE UP CITIZENS OF WASTE
IT'S NOT TOO LATE FOR THE HUMAN RACE
QUESTION WHAT YOU CAN'T SEE
TOXIC WASTE AND MICRO BALLS IN OUR SEAS
CHILDREN ANIMALS AND PLANTS BREATHE
INVISIBLE POLLUTANTS MADE AND DISCARDED
BY YOU AND ME
CITIZENS OF WASTE
QUESTION WHAT YOU CAN'T SEE
QUESTION OUR FOOD
QUESTION OUR ENERGY
QUESTION OUR LIFE
QUESTION OUR HUMANITY
IS THIS OUR FATE
CITIZENS OF WASTE

302

VOLUNTARY WORK
CONDESCENDING ALTRUISM
MORE THAN 35000 VOLUNTEER
FOR ROYAL VOLUNTARY SERVICE
70000 VOLUNTEERS NEEDED
FOR LONDON OLYMPICS
AND 300000 UNPAID WORKERS
NEEDED TO KEEP THE NHS
NATIONAL HEALTH SERVICE
AFLOAT PER DAY
RESPECT TO ALL VOLUNTEERS
BUT YOU ALL OUGHT TO BE PAID

303

MICRO BALLS AND PLASTIC BAGS
PLASTIC TOYS AND PLASTIC CARS
PLASTIC PAINTS AND PLASTIC TRAINS
PLASTIC SHOES AND PLASTIC PLANES
PLASTIC LIMBS AND PLASTIC HIPS
PLASTIC FIBRES AND PLASTIC CHIPS
PLASTIC MONEY AND PLASTIC WAGE
WE ALL LIVE IN THE PLASTIC AGE
WORLDWIDE WAKEUP
PLASTIC WORLD AND SHOUT
WAKE UP WATCH OUT
PLASTICS ALL ABOUT
PLASTIC FOODS BAD
PLASTIC IN OUR FOOD CHAIN
THE BI PRODUCT OF THE
PETRO CHEMICAL AGE
YOUR WELCOME TO
THE PLASTIC AGE

304

IF A SCHOOL IS NOT A FAITH SCHOOL

IS THAT SCHOOL UNFAITHFUL

305

DEMOCRACY FOR SALE

VOTES BOUGHT ON LINE

YOU DON'T HAVE TO DIE TO VOTE

NOW YOU CAN BUY BUY BUY

306

BELIEVERS ARE VERY SUSCEPTIBLE
GULLIBLE PEOPLE
NO PROOF NEEDED JUST
BLIND FAITH
INTELLECTS AND MANUFACTURERS
DEMAND MORE SCIENCE IS TAUGHT
AS SCIENTISTS QUESTION
FOOD FOR THOUGHT

307

WE ARE THE SIXTH LARGEST ECONOMY ON EARTH
AND CONSECUTIVE GOVERNMENTS
HAVE ALLOWED BRITISH SUBJECTS TO LIVE IN POVERTY
WHICH IS WORSE THAN A SAVAGE
WHO KNOWS NOTHING OF WHAT HE IS DEPRIVED OF
EVERY RACE AND GENDER ARE THE HEIRS
OF ALL THE GENERATIONS THAT HAVE LIVED BEFORE
WE ARE ALL THE SUBJECTS OF THEIR
NURTURING KNOWLEDGE
NO MAN OR WOMAN SHOULD LIVE TODAY
WITHOUT CHOICE AND DIGNITY
EVEN SLAVES ARE HOUSED AND FED

308

ONE MUST ACCEPT THAT MAY & HER GOVERNMENT
ARE DEMENTED WITH THEIR DECISION
TO BUILD A NUCLEAR POWER STATION AT
HINKLEY POINT SOMERSET
E.D.F FRANCE WHO HAVE NOT COMPLETED A POWER STATION
IN FINLAND WHICH IS THREE TIMES OVER BUDGET AND
TEN YEARS BEHIND SCHEDULE
A SECOND POWER STATION IN NORMANDY FRANCE IS
TWO TIMES OVER BUDGET AND SIX YEARS BEHIND SCHEDULE
A THIRD POWER STATION IN CHINA THE REACTOR
HAS NEVER WORKED

309

NO ONE LOOKS LIKE
THEMSELVES ANYMORE STOP
SELFI IMAGING USING
PHOTOSHOP

310

DOESN'T IT MAKE YOU THINK
OF ALL THE THINGS YOU COULD BE DOING
IF YOU WEREN'T DOING WHAT YOUR DOING
BESIDES AFTER THE GETTING AWAY FROM IT ALL
IN WARM BREATHABLE FRESH AIR UNCOMPLICATED
AND AFTER AWHILE BORING
THE PHOTOGRAPHER MAYBE
WITH THE LENS FOR AN EYE
LIKE THE DUNGAREES PAINTER
WITH CANVAS TO ADMIRE
SKETCHES AND CARTOONS
WATER COLOURS COME TO LIFE
THE ARTIST WITHIN YOU
LET THEM SEE THE LIGHT
THE MUSICIAN MAYBE
WITH THE EAR FOR THE NOTE
TO COMPOSE WRITE PLAYS
PERFORM SING USE THROAT
THE WRITER MAYBE
WITH WORD SMITH ANALOGY
THE AUTHOR MAYBE
THE JOURNALIST
SPEECH WRITER OR LYRICIST
THERES A WORD FOR THIS
THERES A WORD FOR
EVERYTHING
LET THE POET SHOUT
WITH A PEN MY FRIEND
LET IT ALL OUT

311

COMPROMISE
THE PRIVACY OF A PURCHASED PRIVATE ROOM
JUST TO MAKE YOU THINK

312

LANDLORDS AND COMPETING EMPLOYERS
KEEP POVERTY ALIVE

313

FEAR IS OUR PERPETUAL ENEMY
LOVE IS OUR ETERNAL MEMORY
TRUTH IS OUR WISE COMPANION
PEACE IS OUR FRIEND
CHOICE IS OUR FREEDOM

314

ONE'S LOOKING FOR THE SUN
ONE'S LOOKING FOR A RAINBOW
ONE'S LOOKING FOR A HILL
A MOUNTAIN RIVER OR STREAM
TO DREAM OF
ONE'S LOOKING FOR A STAR
THE MOON OR ANYTHING
THAT MOVES NEAR OR FAR
BEYOND LOOKING FOR A WIFE
OR LOOKING FOR A LIFE
ONE'S LOOKING FOR LOVE

315

BUTTER CUPS AND DAISIES
WOOD LICE AND ANTS
POPPYCOCKS AND PIG TALES
AND FARTS IN YOUR PANTS
LEMONADE BUBBLES
WITH BROWN SAUCE HATS
YELLOW JELLY PYJAMAS
PUMPKIN JAM ROASTED NATS
PEANUT PORRIDGE
STRAWBERRY SOUP
MARMITE MARSHMALLOWS
AND SAUTÉD ROOTS
BANANA SAUSAGE TEA CAKES
ORANGE AND MASH ICED CREAM
PINEAPPLE PICKLED POTATOES
WITH BOILED BROCCOLI BAKED BEANS
ANYONE FOR TEA GRAND CHILDREN

316

LEFT LEFT   LEFT RIGHT LEFT
LABOURS GOT MOMENTUM

317

ONE IS AS OLD AS ONES GUMS
OLDER THAN ONES TEETH
AND WILL LIVE AS LONG
AS ONES HEART BEATS

318

ALL GOD FEARING BELIEVERS MAYBE
IN FOR A NASTY WHOOPS
IF THERE ARE NO PEARLY GATES
NO HEAVEN NO HELL WHOOPS
ON THE OTHER HAND ATHEISTS
ARE IN FOR A GREAT SURPRISE
IF THERE ARE PEARLY GATES
IN HEAVEN WITH HARPS WHOOPS
GET IN WE WIN A PRIZE

319

EACH TIME I HEAR YOUR NAME
MY HEART GOES POP IT HITS MY BRAIN
BLOOD RUSHES ROUND LIKE COCAINE
WOULD ANYONE HERE LIKE TO EXPLAIN
SOMEONE STRAINS
LOVE

320

I CAN'T STOP A RIVERS FLOW
I CAN'T STOP THE RAINS OR SNOW
I CAN'T STOP ANY HURRICANE
I CAN'T STOP LOVING MY WOMAN
I CAN'T STOP THE ICE CAPS MELTING
I CAN'T STOP PEOPLE SWELTERING
I CAN'T STOP A RUNAWAY TRUCK
I CAN'T STOP LOVING YOU ENOUGH
I CAN'T STOP WHAT THE NEIGHBOURS THINK
I CAN'T STOP WHAT IS WRITTEN IN INK
I CAN'T STOP SOCIAL MEDIA LIES
I CAN'T STOP LOVING YOU I'VE TRIED

321

SHE SAYS SHES A MISANTHROPIST

SHE EITHER IS OR SHE'S PISSED

322

IT WAS A FAREWELL JOKE
EVERYONE GAVE THEIR ALL
IT WAS A HOOT
EVERYONE JOINED IN
RIGHT DOWN TO THEIR SKIN
UNTIL THEY REALISED ONE WAS A BLOKE TRING

323

RADICALISATION

IF ONE GAVE YOU LOVE

YOU WOULD BLOW IT

OUT OF ALL PROPORTION

324

THIS PLANET OF OURS
WITH MOUNTAINS SO STEEP
THEY'RE LOST IN OCEANS
OF WATER SO DEEP
WE HAVE TO SEND
MACHINES TO EXPLORE
THE PLANETS AND STARS
AND OUR OCEANS FLOOR
FLYING TO THE STARS
AND SWIMMING WITH FISH
COMPREHENDING THE MEANING
OF THIS LIFE WE WISH
TO SING ABOUT THIS
FOR HOURS AND HOURS
AND APPRECIATE THIS
LIFE OF OURS

325

ONE HAS A NIGHTMARE
ONE NEEDS TO SHARE
THE CLOCKS ARE TICKING
CIVIL UNREST IN AMERICA
RICH OPPOSE POOR
WHITES OPPOSE BLACKS
CIVIL WAR
CLOCKS NEVER CHIME BACK

326

TO SAY
THE GREAT WAR
THE FIRST WORLD WAR
THE ROYAL FAMILY WAR
KING AGAINST KEISER WAR
WAS THE WORST WAR
IS TO BE NATIONALISTIC
FOR HITLERS NAZI WAR
INCLUDING JAPANS EMPERORS WAR
SAW THE GENOCIDE OF
6000000 THATS SIX MILLION JEWS
IN GERMANY ALONE
55000000 THATS FIFTY FIVE MILLION
WORLDWIDE
NEVER MADE IT HOME

327

100 YEARS AGO BRITISH WOMEN DIED TO ENABLE
THEIR FELLOW WOMEN SUFFRAGETTES
TO BE GRANTED BY THE KINGS GOVERNMENT
OF THE DAY THE RIGHT TO VOTE FOR A
POLITICAL PARTY IN A GOVERNMENT ELECTION
IT TOOK TILL 1954 FOR AFRICAN/AMERICANS
AND 1974 FOR THE WOMEN IN SWITZERLAND
TO BE GRANTED THEIR VOTE
THE WORLD AWAITS SAUDI ARABIA
BUT THEIR WOMEN NOW ARE ALLOWED
TO DRIVE CARS
ONE SHOULD BE SHAMED AND FEEL ASHAMED
IF ONE DOES NOT VOTE EITHER THROUGH
LAZINESS OR IGNORANCE OR BOTH
EVERYTHING IN LIFE IS A POLITICAL STATEMENT
OF ONES HUMAN RIGHTS TO LIVE
TO BE HOUSED FED AND EDUCATED
TO WORK FOR THEIR FUTURE AND CREATE
A BETTER COUNTRY
A BETTER WORLD

328

E T E R N I T Y MAKES LIFE SUCK

329

I'VE SEEN MANY SCARECROWS
BUT NEVER A FEMALE ONE
I WITNESSED MY FIRST
IN DOWNING STREET
SHE RESIDES THERE WITH
ANOTHER ONE

330

DACRE & MURDOCH
BARCLAY BROTHERS 2
ARE CORRUPT AS
EACH OTHER
MAYS GOVT TOO

331

IF WE ARE TO BELIEVE IN
GHOSTS AND SPIRITS
THEN THE WORLD MUST BE
OVER ONE HUNDRED FEET
DEEP WITH THEIR APPARITIONS

332

REPETITIVE PRAYERS
LEAVE NO TIME FOR
QUESTIONING

333

WE CAN'T BE EXPECTED
TO PUT THE TOOTHPASTE
BACK IN THE BREXIT TUBE
BORIS JOHNSON MP
BUT WE MUST GET ALL
OUR SYRIAN AND IRAQI
DUCKS BACK IN A ROW

334

VEGANS MAKE AN EDUCATED CHOICE
ONE CHOOSES VEGANISM FOR
MANY REASONS HEALTHY LIFESTYLE
ANIMAL RIGHTS AND WELFARE
ORGANIC SOIL PRESERVATION
NO GMO NO PESTICIDES
NO HERBICIDES AND ALL OTHER BESIDES
CLEAN AIR PURE WATER
KEEP EARTH CLEANER WE OUGHT TO
VEGANS DO NOT EAT ANYTHING
WITH A FACE
PLANET EARTH IS PLANT BASED
TO FEED AND NOURISH ANIMALS
AND THE HUMAN RACE

335

THOSE WHO SMILE WHILE LOOKING UP
TOWARDS THE SKY
THEY PRAY TO GOD WE ARE PUZZLED
AS TO WHY
SOME CALL THEMSELVES SWAMI
OTHERS MULLAHS AND PRIESTS
WE SMILE INTO THEIR FACES
WE'RE ALL SMARMY ATHEISTS

336

TO QUESTION OR NOT TO QUESTION
WHAT IS THE ANSWER
WITHOUT QUESTION
THERE WOULD BE NO ANSWERS WITHOUT QUESTIONS
WE DO NOT EVOLVE
QUESTION THE BLOODY QUESTIONS
SEEK OUT THE INFORMATION THE ANSWERS
THE TRUTH IS OUT THERE

337

WE ARE THE HEIRS OF ALL THE GENERATIONS
THAT HAVE PRECEDED US
SO LOVE EARTH AND ALL LIFE ON THIS
UNIQUE BEAUTIFUL ECOSYSTEM

338

THE KOOKABURRA'S GOING JUST LIKE THE DODO
RIGHT UNDER THE AUSSIES NOSE (THEY KNOW)

339

NUCLEAR FUSION IS A WASTE
OF TIME SPACE AND MONEY
WHICH COULD BE SPENT ON
RENEWABLE ENERGY RESOURCES
THAT ARE CLEAN CONSTANT & SAFE
TO HUMANITY AND PLANET EARTH
A WASTEFUL POWER STATION
BLIGHTING THE SHORELINE OF
SOME PICTURESQUE ESTUARY
A GREY OBSCENE STRUCTURE
MADE OF REINFORCED CONCRETE
SPILT AND SET OVER IRON STEEL
FRAMEWORK TOWERING UP INTO
A BEAUTIFUL BLUE SKYLINE
LIKE SOME UGLY PRE HISTORIC
MISPLACED MONOLITH THAT
BARES NO MEANING NOR RELEVANCE
FOR BEING THERE FOR ALL OUR
CHILDREN'S CHILDREN'S
CHILDREN TO CLEAN UP AND
GET RID OF THE TOXIC
WASTE SET IN MORE CONCRETE
TO DISPOSE OF SOMEWHERE
A TOTAL TOXIC WASTE OF ENERGY

340

EVERY TIME A SPORTS PERSON
LOOKS UP TO THE SKY AND
THANKS THEIR GOD
THEY UNDERMINE THEIR OWN
ACHIEVEMENTS ABILITIES AND
DEDICATION TO TRAINING
AFTER ALL IF THEY TRULY
BELIEVED THEIR GOD INFLUENCES
THEIR PROFESSIONAL ACHIEVEMENTS
THEY NEED NOT TRAIN AT ALL
DISRESPECTING THEMSELVES

341

MEETING PEOPLE SOCIALLY
DRINKING ASTRONOMICALLY HIGH
TAXED FALLING DOWN LIQUIDS
IS NOT ONLY DEPLORABLY SAD
IT IS NOT A PRETTY SIGHT
ALCOHOL IS A CLASS A DRUG
THAT POISONS THE BLOOD
AND CAUSES LIVER DISEASE
AND INEVITABLY DEATH

342

COLOUR ME NOT OF CANARY YELLOW HAIR
COLOUR ME NOT OF CHERRY RED LIPS
COLOUR ME NOT OF TANGERINE SKIN
TINGED BY THE SUN JUST A BIT
COLOUR ME NOT OF SKY BLUE EYES
COLOUR ME NOT OF TURQUOISE NAILS
COLOUR ME NOT OF PURPLE BERRY TOES
ONE CANNOT COLOUR SHADOWS OF RAINBOWS

343

PRIVACY LIMITED TO THE FEW
WHAT PRICE PRIVACY
PRIVILEGED TO WHO
THE ELITE ARE ENTITLED
BEING HONOURED AND FAVOURED
THEY TAKE THEIR ADVANTAGES
WHICH IN TIME MAKES THEM
FEEL IMPORTANT AND SPECIAL
ON THE OTHER SIDE OF PRIVACY
WE HAVE A PRISONER IMPRISONED
CONFINED IN A COOLER
IN A NICK SOMEWHERE
INTERNED INTERNEE HOSTAGE
PRIVACY LIMITED TO THE FEW
PRIVACY PRICELESS

344

SO WHO OWNS THE EARTH THE SKY
AND THE AIR THAT WE ALL BREATHE
WHOSE HUMAN RIGHTS ARE WE
OUT TO DECEIVE
WHAT AND IN WHOSE NAME
ARE WE ALL TO RECEIVE
FRACKING IS THE WORST
KIND OF ENERGY
SO LETS CONSIDER PLANET EARTH
AND WHERE HER ENERGIES LIE
THE WIND IS OBVIOUS
THERE UP IN THE SKY
THE TIDAL SURGE IS CONSTANT
WORLD WIDE WAVES
FRACKING IS THE WORST
ENERGY OF IT'S KIND TODAY
SO WHOSE AUTHORITY MAKES
THESE DECISIONS
THEY ARE JUST HUMAN BEINGS
OUT TO MAKE A KILLING
SOD PLANET EARTH
AND ALL HUMAN BEINGS
FRACKING IS THE WORST KIND OF ENERGY
SO WHAT DOES ONE DO
WITH CONTAMINATED WATER
MILLIONS OF TONS OF
WATER TO BE SORTED
WITH HUNDREDS OF TRUCKS
THE ROADS AROUND WELLS
WILL BE THWARTED
FRACKING IS THE WORST KIND OF ENERGY
IT MUST BE HALTED

345

QUOTE NAPOLEON
DEATH IS NOTHING
BUT TO LIVE DEFEATED
AND GLORIOUS IS TO DIE DAILY
OR LIFE IS EVERYTHING
BUT TO DIE WINNING
AND MISERY IS TO LIVE FOREVER

346

ALL CREATURES ANIMALS MAMMALS
BIRDS INSECTS FISH AND HUMANS
ARE GIVEN THE GIFT OF LIFE
THE PRESENT
CONSCIOUSNESS

347

TOGETHER WE BOTH EMBARK UPON
A JOURNEY OF INADEQUACIES
DISCOVERING OUR STRENGTHS AND
WEAKNESSES AND EMBRACING THE
UNKNOWN EMOTIONS AND MORALS
THAT WILL INEVITABLY ENTWINE TO
BUILD A RELATIONSHIP WITH THE
EMBODIMENT OF LOVE THAT SHALL
FOREVER BE OUR FUTURE

348

SOMETIMES ONE WONDERS WHY ONE'S DEPRESSED
MAYBE IT'S THE QUEEN OR THE LORDS ONE DETESTS
OR THE LAW MAKERS AND THEIR PROCESS
HOW THEY ARE BOUGHT BY THEIR LOBBYISTS
MAYBE IT'S THE RAIN OR NOT ENOUGH SUNSHINE
AND YET ONE LOVES THE FOUR SEASONS EVEN WET
NO IT'S THE LAW AND HOW WE ARE FORCED TO ACCEPT
THE MISINFORMATION ABOUT COWS ONE WILL BET
THE OZONE HOLE WOULD MEND ITSELF
ONLY IF COWS WERE PUT DOWN BY THE VETS

349

TICK TOCK YOUR TIME IS CLOCKED
YOUR BORN YOUR NUMBERED
YOUR TICKED IN A BOX
YOUR NUMBERS MAY CHANGE
EVEN BEFORE YOU ARE NAMED
UNTIL YOUR NATIONAL INSURANCE
NUMBER IS ENGAGED
TICK TOCK THE CALF IS CLOCKED
IT IS BORN IT IS NUMBERED
IT IS TICKED IN A BOX
TICK TOCK THE MALE CALF IS CLOCKED
6 MONTHS TOPS TILL IT'S HEADS CHOPPED OFF
FED ONLY MILK SO IT'S FLESH IS WHITE
THIS IS VEAL YES THIS IS REAL
TICK TOCK THE FEMALE CALF IS CLOCKED
48 MONTHS TILL IT'S HEADS CHOPPED OFF
IN THAT TIME IT IS RAPED A FEW TIMES

HER BABIES TAKEN AWAY SO HER MILK WILL
CONSTANTLY FLOW INTO PLASTIC BOTTLES
THEN OFF TO THE ABATTOIR TO BE
STUNNED SLAUGHTERED THEN BUTCHERED
THEIR FLESH SOLD TO EAT
THEIR SKINS ON THE SOLES OF YOUR FEET
TICK FUCKING TOCK

350

MILK
CALF HORMONE GROWTH FEED
WHY DO HUMANS STILL SUCK COWS TITS

351

HOW CAN EARTH SUSTAIN MANS OBSESSION WITH GROWTH
TO GROW AND TO MAKE ONE HAS TO
DESTROY CONQUER MINE PRODUCE AND MANUFACTURE
TRANSPORTATION OF ALL PRODUCING WASTE AND EATING ENERGY
FROM A GLASS HOUSE WORLD TO A PLASTIC WORLD
WELCOME TO WORLD WIDE WASTE

352

PRIME MINISTER MAY LEFT US IN DISMAY
ANXIOUS DISCOURAGED AND AFRAID
WHY DOES MISS MAY NOT LIKE
THE FOX AND THE ELEPHANT
LIKE ME AND YOU
OH THEY DON’T MAKE GOOD SHOES

353

PIGGY IN THE MIDDLE
HAS NO VOICE OF APPEAL
PIGGY IN THE MIDDLE
YOU CAN ONLY SQUEAL
PIGGY IN THE MIDDLE
VEGANS KNOW YOU CAN FEEL
PIGGY IN THE MIDDLE
YOU ARE A CARNIVORES MEAL
CENTRALIST POLITICIANS
TAKE A STAND IN THE MIDDLE
THEY TAKE A LITTLE RIGHT WING POLICY
AND SELL THEM IN A SOCIALIST WAY
VEGETARIANS PUT THEMSELVES IN THE MIDDLE
OF A CARNIVORE AND A VEGAN
FUSSY CARNIVORES ARE VEGETARIANS
VEGETARIANS ARE JUST FUSSY CARNIVORES

354

BLOW AWAY THE BLUES
JUST READ THE FACTS
YOU VOTE YOU CHOOSE
VOTE THE REDS BACK

355

FUCKING LAWYERS
WORD SMITHS OF LAW
POETIC JUSTICE
PRODUCING ENOUGH
FACTS AND STATEMENTS
AND ANTI VIEWS
TO CREATE DUBIOUS
CONFUSION AND DOUBT
TO BE LEFT TO OTHER
LAWYERS TO SOUGHT
THE BLOODY THING OUT

356

WHEN ONE INFORMS ONES' DOCTOR
ONES' STOPPED TAKING PRESCRIPTION DRUGS
ONE DOES EXPECT A TINY LITTLE RESPECT
ONE DOES NOT EXPECT SILENT STARES NOR HUGS

357

IF ONE DOES NOT VOTE
ONE DOES NOT HAVE A SAY
ONE CANNOT CRITICISE
IN ANYWAY
ONE IS NOT IN THE GAME
ONE DOES NOT HAVE A TICKET
ONE CAN'T COME IN
ONE IS BARRED GO AWAY
ONE GROANS AND MOANS
WITH EVERY MOVE ONE MAKES
ONE IS NEGATIVE UNDISCIPLINED
PROBABLY OVER WEIGHT
ONE ACHIEVES ABSOLUTELY NOTHING
ONES CONTRIBUTIONS ARE NIL
ONE BLAMES THE WHOLE OF SOCIETY
FOR THE WAY ONE FEELS
IGNORANCE IS BLISS
ONE'S HEARD OF THIS
BUT ONE'S NOT HAPPY ONE'S UGLY
YOU ARE THE PROOF OF IT
IF ONE WANTS TO CRITICISE
ONE NEEDS TO CONTRIBUTE
IF ONE FEELS THE NEED
TO SAY ONES PIECE
ONE HAD BETTER
MOVE ONES FAT ARSE
AND BLOODY WELL VOTE

358

YOU THINK YOU ARE A LONER
WHEN YOU PLAY SOLITAIRE
YOU THINK YOU ARE A WINNER
AND YOUR GOING SOMEWHERE
I THINK YOU ARE A LOOSER
AND YOU ARE GOING NOWHERE
AS YOU SIT ON YOUR OWN
PLAYING SOLITAIRE

359

EINSTEIN WAS ASKED
WHAT WEAPONS WILL DECIDE THE OUTCOME
OF A THIRD WORLD WAR
EINSTEIN REPLIED WITH A TWINKLING IN HIS EYE
I DON'T KNOW BUT THE FOURTH
MAY BE WITH STICKS n STONES

360

LIVING IN A SECULAR SOCIETY WITH
SECULAR FRIENDS AND FAMILIES
IF OR WHEN A COUPLE GET HITCHED
AND HAVE CHILDREN THEY MAY WISH
TO ASK FAMILY AND FRIENDS TO BE
ATHEISTS PARENTS FOR
SECULAR GUIDANCE

361

WHEN YOU COME HOME TIRED
AND EXHAUSTED FROM WORK
DO YOU EVER THINK OF THOSE
THAT HAVEN'T AND DON'T
ONE THING ONE LEARNS
LIVING OUT ON THE FARM
THE STRONG SURVIVE
THE WEAKEST ONES
IF ONE HAD ONES WAY
EVERYBODY WOULD EAT
EVERYBODY WOULD SLEEP SAFE
EVERYBODY COULD SPEAK

362

CHOOSE WISELY YOUR COMPANY
CHOOSE WISELY WHERE YOU MEET
CHOOSE THE WISE AND THE FRIENDLY
FOR YOU'LL BECOME THE COMPANY YOU KEEP

363

LIKE TEAR DROPS AND DEW
THE TEARS OF TIME WEEP THROUGH
OVER THE GENOCIDE OF 6
YES SIX MILLION JEWS
SHOULD BE ACKNOWLEDGED COMMEMORATED
AND EDUCATED WORLD WIDE
THE WORLDS UNITED NATIONS
AGREE NO GENOCIDE
YET WE INDOCTRINATE OUR CHILDREN TO BE
DIVISIVE WITH RELIGIOUS BELIEFS
YET WE EDUCATE OUR CHILDREN TO BE
COMPETITIVE AND BETTER THAN THEM
AND WE STILL ENCOURAGE OUR CHILDREN
TO EAT BURGERS AND MILKSHAKES
AND ANYTHING WITH A FACE

364

CARNIVORES AND VEGETARIANS DRINK
CALF HORMONE GROWTH FEED
COWS UDDER TIT MILK
VEGANS DRINK AND ACKNOWLEDGE
ALMOND MILK
COCONUT MILK
FLAX MILK
HAZELNUT MILK
HEMP MILK
OAT MILK
RICE MILK
SOYA MILK
SUNFLOWER MILK
WHOLE GRAIN MILK
AND LOTS MORE HEALTHY
ALTERNATIVES TO COWS
OR ANY OTHER ANIMALS HORMONE GROWTH FEED

365

MANS FIENDISH FRIEND DEPRESSION
IS SELDOM SPENT IN THE COMPANY OF OTHERS
LIKE A SHROUD IT APPEARS WITHOUT INVITATION
AND LEAVES ONLY ONE LONELY
AND FULL OF DESPAIR

366

DRIFT NOT INTO THE DARK RATHER
THE DAWN OF DESIRE AND DREAMS
FEAR IS NOT FAIR
FEAR IS NOT FATE
FEAR IS THE SUBSEQUENCE OF
SUPPRESSION GOD FEARING
BULLYING AND HATE
SEE THROUGH THE LIES
SEE THROUGH THE APATHY
SEARCH OUT THE TRUTH
AND THE FAKE FROM REALITY
APATHY INDOCTRINATED BY RELIGIONS
THEN EMPOWERED BY LAW
AND ENFORCED BY GOVERNMENTS
PEOPLE ARE EQUAL

367

C H R I S T M E S S
C H R I S T M E S S E S WITH turkey A R S E H O L E S

368

ATHEISTS DO NOT JUDGE NOR BLAME
THE CARNIVORES INDOCTRINATED WAYS
WHEN ONE HAS ONLY KNOWN EATING
THE FLESH FROM CREATURES AND
SPECIES WITH FACES
WE'RE HERE TO SUPPORT AND TO EXPLAIN
BEING VEGAN ONE BECOMES ONES HEALTHIEST
SO TOO SHALL EARTH AGAIN

369

ONE KNOWS WHEN
UNCLES BILL JACK AND ARTHUR
AUNTIES LIL MAUDE AND MARTHA
GRANDPA SINGS WITH GRANDMA WILMA
ALL THE KIDS ARE SCREAMING LAUGHTER
WITH NODDY HOLDER AND ROY WOOD
BEING PLAYED EVERYWHERE IN THE NEIGHBOURHOOD
GATHER AROUND THE BIGGEST TABLE
PULL THE CRACKERS AND WEAR THE HATS
ONE KNOWS NOW WHAT DAY IT IS
IT'S CHRISTMAS
THE INDOCTRINATED FESTIVE HOLIDAY FOR CHRISTIANS SEDUCING

ALL THEIR BELIEVERS FOR OVER 2000 Yrs TO CELEBRATE THEIR
SYMBOL OF TORTURE WITH A HUMAN NAILED
TO THE CROSS USING 3 NAILS
AND TOASTING THIS CHRISTIAN HOLYDAY WITH THE HOLY WATERS
TURNED INTO WINE AND THERE YOU HAVE IT
THE WORLD HAS BEEN AWASH WITH ALCOHOLICS
EVER SINCE FERMENTING BREWING AND DISTILLING
STILL BELIEVING

370

PLASTIFICATION
LOOK AT THE WORLD
WHAT DOES ONE SEE
ENDLESS REPETITION
ENDLESS REPLICATION
ENDLESS SUFFOCATION
OF PLANET EARTHS
LAND AIR & SEAS

371

WITNESS NOT WHO DICTATES
WITNESS NOT WHOM EXTERMINATES
WITNESS NOT HATE
WITNESS THEIR FATE
WITNESS THEIR HUMANITY
WITNESS THEIR SILENCE
WITNESS THEIR DEATHLY SILENCE
REMEMBER PEACE

372

EAT MEAT AT YOUR PERIL
ESPECIALLY CHICKEN COWS AND PIGS
THEN DO NOT FORGET THE FISH
THEY CONSUME HALF THE WORLDS
ANTIBIOTICS
YES FISH FARMS CHICKEN FARMS
PIG FARMS AND COWS
THEY'RE ALL SICK ILL
AND UNHEALTHY NOW
THE GREED TO FEED
AT THEIR DIGNITY
THEIR PAIN
THEIR DEATH
MAYBE TO THE DETRIMENT
OF ONES' OWN LAST BREATH

373

SAVE THE PLANET ANY WHICH WAY ONE CAN
EVER SINCE I WAS YOUNG I HAVE LOVED AND RESPECTED
NATURE AND ANIMALS I DON'T EAT THEM I AM VEGAN
RAVE FREEDOM TO VOTE TO HAVE A SAY
TO SCREAM AND SHOUT TO SING OUT LOUD
TO DANCE ALL DAY JUST TO LET IT ALL OUT
SHARE SOME LOVE IT IS NOT A CRIME
TO HAVE A NICE DAY AND SOME PEACE OF MIND
AND RAVE ONE MUST BE BRAVE
TO RAVE & SAVE FACE
ESPECIALLY THE BILLIONS OF ANIMALS
MAMMALS FISH AND BIRDS
EATEN EVERY SINGLE DAY

374

MILLIONS OF FINGERS TALKING
WORDSWORTH ON LINE
WAR & PEACE LOVE & CRIME
THUMBS TEXT OVERTIME

375

JUST BECAUSE IT'S LEGAL
DOES NOT MEAN IT'S GOOD FOR YOU
IT CERTAINLY DOES NOT MAKE IT RIGHT
IT MAY POSSIBLY ADDICT AND KILL YOU
IT IS HARMFUL SHIT
BUT IT IS TAXED AND LEGAL ALRIGHT

376

CHOICE IS FREEDOM
FREEDOM TO CHOOSE
CHOICE TO CHOOSE
WHATEVER YOU SEE WHATEVER YOU DO
CHOICE IS YOUR VOICE
VOICE YOUR CHOICE
DON'T BE A SHEEP BE A GOAT
MAKE THE SIGN OF THE CROSS MATTER
USE WISELY AND
GET OUT THERE AND VOTE

377

BORN A PEACE BABY
IN THE PLASTIC AGE
BECOMING PLASTIC PEOPLES
LITTERALLY
SUFFOCATING THE WORLD WITH PLASTIC WASTE

378

THE GREATEST HUMANITARIAN SERVICE
ON THE PLANET WORKS
THE NATIONAL HEALTH SERVICE
IT IS PRECISELY THAT THE N H S WORKS
IS WHY IT HAS BEEN UNDER CONSTANT
ATTACK BY PRIVATISATION EVER SINCE
IT WAS CONCEIVED BY NYE BEVAN
DUBIOUS DEALS SLY DEALS AND
BACK DOOR DEALS
HAMMERED HUMOROUSLY HOME BY
HASSLING DRUG DEALERS FROM
DRUG COMPANIES CALLING THEMSELVES
PHARMACEUTICALS
AND STILL THE HUNT GOES ON
TO MAKE A KILLING OUT OF THE NHS
THE BRITISH NATIONAL HEALTH SERVICE
LIVES AND WORKS AND
DESERVES THE BEST
SOCIALISTS

379

TO QUESTION OBSESSION
MAYBE TO QUESTION DEDICATION

380

THE SYSTEM IS BROKE
THE INVESTMENT BUBBLE HAS CHOKED
THE WHOLE WORLD INTO A FINANCIAL JOKE
AS THIS PLASTIC WORLD SMOTHERS AND CHOKES
THE LIFE OUT OF ALL LIVING CREATURES HERE
ON OUR BEAUTIFUL PLANET EARTH

381

A COW IS ALLOWED MORE WATER THAN YOU
A COW IS ALLOWED MORE ANTIBIOTICS THAN YOU
A COW SEEMS TO HAVE MORE RIGHTS THAN YOU
BUT THEN THE COW DOES GET
TO BE EATEN BY YOU CARNIVORES

382

A HORSE AND QUEEN
THE SPORT OF KINGS
HORSES FOR COURSES
TIS JUST GAMBLING IT SEEMS
HOW MUCH WATER
HOW MUCH FEED
HOW MUCH ANTIBIOTICS
TO RIDE RACE GAMBLE AND BREED
NO TAX NEEDED NOR
INSURANCE FOR A HORSE
TO RIDE THE QUEENS HIGHWAY
OH IT'S THE QUEENS OF COURSE

383

MENTAL HEALTH SOLD
TO US ON TELLY
PHARMACEUTICALS CAN CONTROL
BIPOLAR REALLY
THEY CAN BE HEART SURGEONS
AND BRAIN SURGEONS
SOME EVEN SUFFER
WITH DEPRESSION
THE PEOPLE I KNOW
WITH BIPOLAR AGREE
BRAIN SURGERY HEART SURGERY
EVEN TREE SURGERY THEY JEST
NEVER TRUST THE PHARMACEUTICAL
DRUG BARONS INTERESTS

384

ALICE HAWKINS DIED 100yrs AGO
FOR EQUALITY OF GENDER PAY AND VOTE
QUEEN ELIZABETH HAS REIGNED FOR 65yrs
PATRONISING ALL HER FEMALE SUBJECTS
IN THEIR PASSIVE SUBMISSIVE ROLES
TERESA MAY & AMBER RUDD BOTH
SERVED & SERVING HOME SECRETARIES
AND PRIME MINISTER FOR THE LAST 5yrs
IN THIS CONSERVATIVE GOVERNMENT
HAVE ACHIEVED ABSOLUTELY NOTHING
FOR EQUAL GENDER PAY
QUEEN EII THATCHER AND MAY
SHOULD HAVE DEMANDED THEIR GENDER SAY

385

THEY WILL ALL STAY FOREVER YOUNG
AS LONG AS THERE ARE
PICTURES AND FILMS OF THE PAST
AS LONG AS THEIR MEMORIES AND STORIES LAST
AS LONG AS THEIR PHOTOGRAPHS
APPEAR BEHIND GLASS
AS LONG AS THEIR GREATNESS
AND LOVE SURPASS
THEY WILL ALL STAY FOREVER YOUNG

386

REMEMBER THE PAST
YOUR EXPERIENCES
AND KNOWLEDGE
IS YOUR PRESENT
TO YOUR FUTURE
GENEALOGY

387

THERE WAS A YOUNG MAN FROM LIMERICK
WHOSE ART IT WAS TO MIMIC
AS QUICK AS A FLASH
ONE IS MESMERISED BY HIS TACT
TO VANISH ALONG WITH YOUR WALLET

388

THIS IS MY ART
IT IS NOT SOLD
MY DREAMS WRITTEN & SUNG
MY STORIES TOLD

389

IF IT WASN'T FOR GOD
ONE WOULDN'T BE AN ATHEIST
ONE WOULDN'T WORRY ABOUT
WHAT HAPPENS BEHIND CLOSED
MONASTERY DOORS OF NON
TAXPAYING CHARITIES LIKE
RELIGIONS
IF ONE BELIEVED IN KARMA
ONE WOULD BE WORRIED ABOUT
YOU

390

CITIZENS OF WASTE
IT IS THE TIME TO FACE
THIS PLASTIC WORLD OF OURS
IS A DISASTROUS DISGRACE
PARASITIC PARTICLES OF
PLASTIC POLLUTANTS
POISONING PLANT BASE LIFE
MARINE AND GREEN
IT IS UP TO ALL OF US
TO KEEP PLANET EARTH CLEAN

391

ONE KNOWS WHAT IS RIGHT
ONE KNOWS WHAT IS WRONG
SPEAK TO ONES NEIGHBOUR
STAND TOGETHER BE STRONG
SPEAK AS ONE CONNECTIVE CHOICE
SPEAK AS ONE COLLECTIVE VOICE
SPEAK TO THOSE AND OFFER THEM CHOICE
SPEAK TO THOSE AND GIVE THEM A VOICE

392

MEAT COCKTAILS BACK IN VOGUE FROM
DETROIT USA 1952 £28 A GLASS
MEAT STOCK FOR TOFFS
AND ALCOHOLIC CARNIVORES

393

ONE MUST REITERATE
EVEN REGURGITATE THE FACT
COUNCIL TAX IS A
TAX ON THE TAXED

394

COMPETITION PRODUCES LOSERS
DOES THAT DEFINE LOSERS COMPETE
RUNNING & CYCLING IN CIRCLES
RUNNING & CYCLING ON ROADS
SWIMMING ROWING AND CANOEING
YACHTING SAILING TO AND FRO
THE DEDICATION & SELF DISCIPLINE
THE PAINS & STRAINS OF TRAINING SHOW
THEY COULD ALL BE PUT TO BETTER USE
CREATING AND PRODUCING
SOMETHING LIKE CHARGING PHONES
OTHER THAN SNOW

395

SPORT USED TO BE FUN
UNTIL SPORT WAS BOUGHT
NOW SPORT CHARGES
SPORT'S NOT SPORTING
FOOD FOR THOUGHT

396

ONE USED TO DREAM
AFTER ONE CLOSED ONE'S EYES
PEOPLE LIVING AND PULLING AS ONE
PEOPLE HAVING FUN
ONE USED TO DREAM
WHEN ONE CLOSED ONES EYES
COLOURFUL PEOPLES SHARING
THEIR COLOURFUL LIVES
ONE USED TO DREAM
ABOUT NO RELIGIOUS TIES
NO POLITICAL LIES
NO REASON TO OSTRACISE
ONE USED TO DREAM
AFTER ONE SWITCHED OFF THE LIGHT
ONE USED TO DREAM THROUGH THE DAY
NOT JUST THROUGH THE NIGHT

397

TRUST
TRUST IS HAVING CONFIDENCE
IN SELF OR OTHERS
A POSITION OF TRUST IS THE
CONFIDENCE ONE HAS IN THAT PERSON
AND A TRUST IS ARRANGED WITH A
CONFIDENCE IN A FIRM OR COMPANY
OF LAWYERS AND SOLICITORS TO
WHOM MONIES SHALL BE DISPATCHED
SENT PAID OR OTHERWISE OR WAYS

TO PARTICULAR DEPENDENTS AND
PARTICIPATING PERSONS
TRUST HAS NOTHING
NOTHING TO DO WITH RELIGION
RELIGION HIGH JACKED TRUST
THOUSANDS OF YEARS AGO
ALONG WITH FAITH AND BELIEF
TRUST IS CONFIDENCE
IN SELF OR WITH OTHERS

398

ALL LIFE AND EVERYTHING ON IT IS
DEVALUED
WHEN MAN PUTS A PRICE ON IT

399

I ONCE THOUGHT
A BIRD OF PARADISE
WAS PEEING ON MY KNEE
IT WAS NOT UNTIL I LOOKED CLOSER
I'D SPILT MY CUP OF TEA

400

BOLLOCKS
WHAT A LOAD OF RUBBISH
IN GARBAGE BAGS FROM
JOHN O GROATS TO LANDS END
TO LONDON AND BACK UP TO
SCOTLAND
RUBBISH RUBBISH EVERYWHERE
WE ARE ALL RESPONSIBLE
FOR WHAT WE THROW AWAY
CITIZENS OF WASTE
EACH AND EVERYONE
OF US HAVE BECOME
LETS BE RESPONSIBLE
PLASTIC AGE PEOPLE
AND ELIMINATE PLASTIC
FOREVER FROM
OUR BEAUTIFUL
PLANET EARTH

401

IN THIS WORLD OF STRAWS
WE ALL LIVE IN
BEING CONSCIOUS OF WHAT
WE SUCK IN
AND WHAT WE BLOW OUT
WHAT WE ARE SUCKED INTO
AND WHAT WE'RE BLOWN
OUT WITH
IN THE SHORT N LONG OF LIFE
SIZE REALLY DOES MATTER
YOUR CHOICE TO DRAW
THE SHORT STRAW
OR THE LONG STRAW
IT ALL DEPENDS
WHO'S CHOOSING
THE BLUE FEW OR
THE REDDY MANY

402

CRITICISM IS WELCOMED
WHEN FAIR AND HONEST
TO CRITICISE
WITH BIAS AND LIES
IS NOT

403

THERE IS A WILL
THERE IS A PILL
WHICH ONE WOULD YOU
PREFER TO SPILL
A LIVING LIE
IS A DEAD MANS EYE
WHO CANNOT READ BETWEEN THE LINES
AND TRUTH DESERVES
HER STORY IS
HER STORY
HIS STORY IS
HIS STORY
HISTORY IN THE MAKING
FILMED AND RECORDED
REALITY SHOWING SOCIAL
MEDIA LIVING LIFE BEING
STREAMED ON EVERY
SCREEN
THERE IS A WILL
THERE IS A PILL
WHICH ONE WOULD YOU
PREFER TO SWALLOW

404

MAY YOU HAVE GONE
TOO FAR RIGHT
LEFT TO OUR LION
LABOURS BRIAN MAY

405

OPPOSITION
OPPOSING ARMIES ARGUMENTS
STAND POINTS VIEWS OPINIONS
AND RELIGIOUS BELIEFS OF COURSE
A DICTATORIAL OPPOSITION
PERSONNEL ARE TERRORISTS AND ACTIVISTS
THEY FOUND HIM GUILTY CRUCIFIED HIM
AND IN RIDICULING HIM THE ROMANS
FINALLY TURNED THIS SON OF A MAGICIAN
INTO A SAINT
USING HIS MAGICAL HOLY WATERS TO
WINE AND DINE THE REST OF THE WORLD
ON IT'S MAGICAL TAXABLE PROFITABLE
POPULARITY FOR THE POPULOUS
PROVIDING THEM WITH PATIENCE
BUT LESS PASSIVE PERSISTENT
PISS UPS PRESENTING THE NHS A&E
SELF HARMING ALCOHOLIC PATIENTS UNNECESSARILY

406

THE WORSHIPFUL COMPANY OF BUTCHERS GUILD
WHAT IS WORSHIPFUL ABOUT A COMPANY OF BUTCHERS
RELIGIOUS TRAITS OF SACRIFICIAL
LAMBS CALVES AND GOATS
ARE ALL THE ELECTRONIC CAPTIVE STUN GUNS BLESSED
ALONG WITH ALL THE SAWS BLADES & KNIVES
THAT SLAUGHTER MILLIONS OF LIVES
THEY BUTCHER WITH NO SORROW
WHERE RIVERS OF BLOOD FLOW
WHERE EVERY MAN KNOWS
HIS DAYS WORK HE TAKES HOME
TO HIS WIFE HIS CHILDREN
HIS DOGS AND HIS PONY
YES THEY PAY THE VETS
THESE BUTCHERS WHO LOVE THEIR PETS

407

VEGETARIANS
CENTRALIST EATERS OR
FUSSY CARNIVORES
DO YOU TRUST
THE ANIMALS AND FISH
YOU EAT ARE HEALTHY
AND HUMANELY BRED
FOR THEIR MEATS
FOR YOU ARE
WHAT YOU EAT
AND THINK
WHAT YOU DRINK

408

HENRIETTA LACKS
NOTHING BUT DIGNITY
FOR HER AND HER FAMILY
AND RECOGNITION FOR
HER HUMAN CELLS TO BE
THE FIRST AND ONLY TO LIVE
OUTSIDE THE HUMAN BODY
BACK IN 1951 IN THE USA
WHEN AN AFRICAN/AMERICAN
WAS NOT TREATED FREELY
FAIRLY NOR EQUAL
THEY LABELED HENRIETTA'S
CELLS AS HELEN LANE FOR
MANY DECADES
HENRIETTA LACKS HUMAN CELLS
HAVE BEEN MULTIPLIED
BOUGHT AND SOLD WORLDWIDE
FOR MEDICAL SCIENCE & RESEARCH
FROM DAY ONE AND STILL UNIQUELY
USED DAILY AND STILL NO COMPENSATION
FOR THE LEGACY CELLS OF
HENRIETTA LACKS
DARE MANKIND PUT A PRICE
ON ONE HUMAN CELL

409

SHE WORE A BROWN FELT HAT
THAT SHE BORROWED
FROM A HORSE IN HACKNEY
AND THE BLOND WIG
LOOKED LIKE SPAGHETTI
THAT CAME FROM THAT LOCALITY
HER BROWN TWEED SUIT WAS SHIFTY
MIDI COAT AND TURN UPS
A BELT SHE BOUGHT WITH BUTTERCUPS
AND RED BOOTS SHE SWAPPED FOR HERS
IN TAMANRASSET SHE LOOKED
QUITE WISE AND READY
NOT LARGE FAT OR HEAVY
MEN TO HER WERE JELLY
HER GIRLFRIENDS FOUND HER BOLD
I FOUND HER VERY COLD
INSIDE A MIXED UP MIND
A HEART THAT WAS FULL OF LOVE
TO GIVE TO ANYONE
WHO COULD BUT GIVE HER TIME
TO SOUGHT OUT HER MIND
WITHOUT GIVING HER YOURS
AS I DID AND LOST THE CAUSE
SHE MUST HAVE FOUND ME COLD
I FOUND HER VERY BOLD
WITH LEWIS CARROLL BOOK IN HAND
SHE WAS QUITE A WOMAN
SO IF ONE SEES HER AROUND
TELL HER TO CALL ROUND
THERES A GUY THERE WITHOUT
A MIND BUT WITH LOVE NO DOUBT

410

THE 2018 MORALS AND EMPATHY
IN THE SAUDI ARABIAN KINGDOM AND
PRINCIPALITIES OF CROWN PRINCE AND
PRINCES HAVE ALLOWED WOMEN
THEIR WOMEN TO DRIVE CARS
BUT IF THEIR WOMEN ALLOW
THEMSELVES TO BE RAPED
THEIR WOMEN ARE THRASHED
YES THRASHED WITH 200 LASHES
AND WAIT FOR IT IMPRISONED
THEN QUESTIONED FOR THEIR MORALS
BUT IF ONE IS A DISSIDENT MALE
SAUDI JOURNALIST
ONE HAD BETTER NOT SPEAK OUT OR
ONE SHOULD FIND ONESELF ON THE
CROWN PRINCES HIT LIST AND
ONE MUST NEVER FORGET
THE 20th CENTURY PRINCESS

411

DEAD FLESH

OR

FRESH VEGETABLES

412

OWEN JONES OUR ORWELL
AUTHOR WRITER AND ORATOR OF OUR TIMES
VERBALLY ABUSED OUTSIDE PARLIAMENT
BY A GANG OF RIGHT WING YOUTHS
ESCORTED BY POLICE
IN FULL PUBLIC VIEW
IS THIS THE BRITAIN WE WANT
RIGHT WING FASCIST CAPITALISTS
WITH EVERYONE FOR THEMSELVES
OR SOCIALISM
WHERE EVERYONE IS CARED FOR
FED AND HOUSED

413

COMPARE HIM NOT TO MANDELA
WHO LED HIS PEOPLE FROM APARTHEID
COMPARE HIM NOT TO GANDHI
WHO LED HIS PEOPLE TO FREEDOM
COMPARE HIM NOT TO ANY MAN
WHO HAS HAD BLOOD ON HIS HANDS
COMPARE HIM TO ONESELF WITH
EXTRAORDINARY SOCIAL INSIGHT & COMPOSURE
SPEAKING TO ALL OPPOSITION HERE & ABROAD
SNP PLAID CYMRU DUP IRA PALESTINE IRAN
ISRAEL TURKEY SAUDI ARABIA SYRIA PAKISTAN
EUROPE PUTIN KIM DON AND MAY
HE JEREMY CORBYN LEAD A SOCIAL GOVERNMENT
BACK TO PARLIAMENT
AND GIVE THE PEOPLE BACK THEIR SAY

414

NOW WE ALL KNOW AND BELIEVE
POLLUTANTS IN OUR AIR WE BREATHE
WELL HOW ABOUT LIGHT POLLUTION
SUN AND ELECTRICITY LIGHTS
WHICH BRINGS ONE ONTO NOISE POLLUTION
DIGITAL DATA MATRIX WORLDS OF WI FI
WHITE NOISE AND DARK NET LOGARITHMS
TO A ROCKET LAUNCHING ANOTHER SATELLITE
AIR NOISE AND LIGHT POLLUTION

415

WE HAVE HAD QUEENS AND PRINCESSES
DUCHESSES BARONESSES DAMES &
LADIES YOU HAVE SAID & DONE
NOTHING FOR YOUR GENDER
FOR OVER A THOUSAND YEARS
INCLUDING PM's THATCHER & MAY
AND QUEEN E TOO
THE SUFFRAGETTES WOMENS DEEDS
LED BY EMMELINE PANKHURST FROM 1903
DESERVE THE TITLES SOME DIED TO GET
THE WOMENS DEEDS OF EQUALITY RIGHTS
THE SUFFRAGETTES
DARE ANYONE REMOVE HER STATUE
PARLIAMENTS SUFFRAGETTE

416

FRACKING SENSE A MYTH
THERE IS NO SENSE IN FRACKING SINCE
BRITISH SHALE GEOLOGICALLY TOO YOUNG
LESS GAS MORE COSTS
LESS PROFITS MORE WASTE
FRACKING SENSE A WASTE OF SPACE
TIME ENERGY AND AN OBSCENE AMOUNT
OF PRECIOUS FRESH WATER TURNED INTO
FRACKING TOXIC WASTE
POISONING LAND WILD LIFE LIVE-STOCK AND
HUMANS BOILS LESIONS AND TUMOURS
GROWING ON THE INSIDE
GROWING ON THE OUTSIDE
GROWING BECAUSE OF FRACKING
FRACKING A TOXIC WASTE OF TIME ENERGY AND SPACE

417

LIGHT OMITTING ORGANISMS

OVER SEVEN MILLION YEARS OLD

SHAKE AND THEY LIGHT UP

LETS GET THESE BABIES TO LIGHT UP OUR WORLD

418

LEFT OVERS
WHATS THAT ALL ABOUT
LEFT OVERS OF WHAT
LEFT OVERS ARE PLURAL
THERES MORE THAN ONE OF THEM
LEFT DOES THAT MEAN
THEY'RE A LEFTY
THEY LEAN TO THE LEFT
A LEFT OVER
NOT RIGHT OVER
BUT LEFT OVER
SOCIALLY OVER
OVER WHAT
OVER THE TOP
OVER THE HILL
OVER THE BRINK
OVER THE EDGE
OVER ANXIOUS
OVER WEIGHT
OVER & OVER
ONE ASKS ONESELF IS IT CRICKET

419

IT'S PROBABLY NOT THE ONE
YOU HAVEN'T MET LOVE
MORE LIKELY IT'S THE ONE
YOU CAN'T FORGET TO LOVE

420

ONES HAIR WILL CHANGE
ONES COMPLEXION TOO
WITH FURROWED FOREHEAD
AND A CHIN OR TWO
ONES EYES AND ONES SMILE
YES ONES SMILING EYES
ARE UNIQUE TO EACH INDIVIDUAL
MAN WOMAN AND CHILD

421

WHO WOULDN'T LIKE TO FLY
LIKE A BIRD UP IN THE DAYLIGHT
JUST GLIDING ON THE AIR
THERES NO BOUNDARIES UP THERE
JUST A WORLD OF SKY
UP THERE IN THE SUNLIGHT
CATCHING FLIES AND APHIDS FREELY
PICKING UP THE THERMALS EASILY
CLIMBING HIGHER
ONE CAN SEE SO CLEARLY
TO FEEL THE AIR
TO FEEL THE BREEZE
TO FEEL THE WIND BENEATH YOUR WINGS
TO HARNESS THAT ENERGY
AND ENGINE POWER RELEASED
TO INTUITIVELY RESPOND TO THESE ELEMENTS
IS REMARKABLE TO ME

422

I LOOK BACK WITH RESPECT
REMEMBERING WHAT MY FATHER LIVED THROUGH
CHANGING UMBRELLAS TO BECOME CHRISTIAN
FROM ONE BEING A JEW
FIGHTING MORE THAN FASCIST ANTI SEMITISM
BUT GENOCIDE TOO
LYING SHROUDS OF UNTOLD FAKE VIEWS
RELIGIONS DIVIDE SEPARATE & CONFUSE

423

CITIZENS OF WASTE
WE NOW HAVE WASTE IN SPACE
4000 DISCARDED SATELLITES
ORBITING THIS PLACE
EARTHS HUMAN INHABITANTS
ARE IT'S WORST OCCUPYING RACE
MINING BURNING POISONING POLLUTING
SUFFOCATING STOP THIS
THIS IS WHAT OUR CHILDREN FACE

424

WOMEN IN THE WORLD WITHOUT EQUALITY

WITHOUT DIGNITY AND HUMAN RIGHTS

GENDER WAGE EQUALITY

WOMEN DESERVE EQUAL RIGHTS

425

ONE REMEMBERS THE MILKMAN DELIVERING

FROM HIS HORSE AND CART

IT WAS THE EARLY 1950's AND ONE CAN VIVIDLY RECOLLECT

THE SMELL OF THE HORSES SHIT AND FART

426

VEGANS DON'T DRINK

THE UDDER MILK

427

THE MORE ONE EXPLAINS
THE LESS TRUTH SPOKEN

428

FREEDOM OF SPEECH
FREEDOM OF CHOICE
FREEDOM TO CHOOSE
NOT TO BE A JEW
NOT TO BE A CHRISTIAN
OR A MUSLIM
NOR RELIGIOUS LIKE YOU
BEING AN ATHEIST
DOES NOT MAKE ONE
ANTI CHRISTIAN ANTI MUSLIM ANTI SEMITIC
IT MAKES ONE ANTI YOUR RELIGIOUS BELIEFS
AND VIEWS ON LIFE

429

21st CENTURY SUFFRAGETTES SUGGEST
21st CENTURY MEN MARCH FOR THEIR GENDER
HOW ABOUT PROSTRATE CANCER
BOLLOCKS!

430

THE 22nd CENTURY IS WHERE
THE ACTIONS GOING TO BE
PREDICTABLE ANALYSTS SEE
THE END OF LIFE ON EARTH IT SEEMS
MANS ARROGANT OBSESSION
TO EVOLVE IS JUST GREED
WHILST THE BILLIONAIRE FEW
WHO LEAVE A SCORCHED ACIDIC EARTH TO
MARS AWAITS FOR THE NEW ARROGANT
WASTES IN SPACE
IF THEY TAKE THEIR DIVISIVE BELIEFS
LIFE ON MARS AS ON EARTH
SHALL BE A REPEAT
OH YES A BILLIONAIRE WASTE OF SPACE
HAS ALREADY GOT A DIGITAL A I GOD IN PLACE

431

ELEPHANTS ARE HARD TO FOLLOW

ELEPHANTS ARE EVEN HARDER TO SWALLOW

432

SOME PEOPLES IN ASIA
BREED DOGS TO EAT
HOW CRUEL AND INHUMANE
THEY SHOULD BREED SHEEP

433

I MAKE THINGS UP
STANDING UP
I CAN'T MAKE THINGS UP
LYING
I STAND
TO MAKE THINGS UP
REALLY I DO
I DO NOT LIE
LYING ABOUT IMAGINATION
DOES NOT STAND UP
I CAN'T STAND
LYING

434

I FEEL LIKE A NERVE
IN A CURRENT SYSTEM
TRAVELLING AT SPEEDS
YET I'M NOT MOVING
I AM IN CONTROL
THERE AGAIN I'M NOT
SHAKES AND TREMBLES
QUIVERING COLD OR CLAMMY HOT
AS MY LIMBS AND LIPS TIGHTEN
LIKE A SAIL TO A MAST
PLEASE REMEMBER THE NERVE
BEHIND THE MASK

435

SUCK THE TOXINS
CHOKE THE FUMES IN
WE'RE ALL SUFFOCATING FROM
CHEMICAL WASTE DEPOSITS
RUBBER TYRES TO VEHICLE EXHAUSTS
TRAINS & RAILWAYS TO AIRPORTS
AEROSOLS TO AEROPLANES
PLASTIC BLEACH & DETERGENTS
TO HAZARDOUS CHEMICAL WASTES
WHEREVER ONE BREATHES
WHEREVER ONE EATS
THE LIVESTOCK HERDS
BRED FOR THEIR MEATS
IT'S IN THE FOOD CHAIN
IT'S OUT THERE EVERYWHERE
IT'S ONLY TIME
AND THERES PLENTY OF IT'S
OUT THERE

436

SCREENING SCREENING
EVERYBODYS STREAMING
STREAMING DATA IN AND
OUT OF THEIR SCREENS
FACE TO FACE FONES
EAR TO EAR FONES
EARTH TO SATELLITE HOMES
BUT I'M JUST STANDING HERE

437

AFTER SETTING AN EXAMPLE FOR ALL OTHERS TO FOLLOW
THE GOVERNMENT & PARLIAMENT
CANNOT CRITICISE THE QUEENS SUBJECTS BEHAVIOUR
DARE THEY

438

CHLORINE CHEMICAL FACILITIES BOMBED IN SYRIA
CHICKEN NUGGETS PIECES WASHED IN CHLORINE CHEMICALS
BEEF MEATS CLEANSED & RINSED IN CHLORINE CHEMICALS
TEETH BRUSHED & WASHED IN CHLORINE WATER
AND ONE BATHES IN CHLORINE WATERS
SO ONE CAN BATHE IN CHLORINE WATERS
ONE CAN EAT & DIGEST CHLORINE MEATS
BUT ONE CANNOT BREATH CHLORINE AIR
WHY CHLORINE AT ALL

439

THREE WORLD WISE WOMEN
WERE EACH GIVEN A SCREEN
WORLD WISE WOMAN ONE
FELL IN LOVE WITH HER OWN REFLECTION
ERECTED STATUES AND PHOTOS OF HERSELF EVERYWHERE
BUT NOTHING CHANGED
WORLD WISE WOMAN TWO
HATED HER IMAGE AND
WAS FOREVER CHANGING
WORLD WISE WOMAN THREE
CONVERSED DEBATED AND SPOKE FREELY TO THE SCREEN
EVERY DAY ABOUT THAT WHICH MUST BE CHANGED
AND THAT WHICH CANNOT BE CHANGED AND TO BE
WISE ENOUGH TO KNOW THE DIFFERENCE

440

THE HUMAN RACE HAS BEEN PLAGUED
WITH A BELIEF SYSTEM SO DIVISIVE
NOT ONLY CAN THEY
THE THREE MAIN ACTS
NOT PROVE GOD EXISTS
THEY CANNOT EVEN AGREE
ON GODS NAME
SO WAR EXISTS IN THE NAME OF GOD

441

SOME BILLIONAIRE WITH A RIGHTEOUS EGO
HAS SET HIMSELF UP AS WAIT FOR IT
AI GOD ONE JESTS NOT
ALREADY AI ROBOTS ARE FUCKED
HOWS THAT FOR INTELLIGENCE

442

EYE CATCHING WHISPERS

POSTURING GESTURES

LOVE EMPATHY AND COMPASSION

SHADOWS OF ONES PLEASURES

443

SHE WAS AS TIMID AS A TIGER
AND AS BOLD AS A PUSSY CAT
SHOES WORN FOR DANCE
BOOTS WORN TO BASH
SCARVES WORN FOR COLOUR
HATS WORN TO FASHION
THE HEADY HEARTS OF ALL STREETS
WHERE THE TALK TALK
IS OF THE WALK WALK
BY THE LADY
EVERYBODY WANTS TO MEET & GREET

444

SHOOT ME NOW
TAKE YOUR SHOT
YOU ALL HAVE A CAMERA
IN YOUR POCKET DO YOU NOT
BIG BROTHER WATCH
YES POLICE WATCH
JUST AS THEY DID
IN THE HILLSBOROUGH BOTCH
A I WATCH YOU SUBJECTS
WITH FACIAL RECOGNITION
IT IS FAR FROM PERFECT
AND YOU COULD END UP IN PRISON
CIVILIANS WE ARE NOT
WALKING I D CARDS TO SPOT
WE WILL ALL BE CRIMINALS
TO PROVE WE ARE NOT
PRIVATISATION PEELS AWAY
THE POSTER PLACARDS
REVEALING THEIR TRUE EYES
BEHIND THE ESTABLISHMENTS MASKS

445

RELIGION HAS NO HUMOUR
THERE'S NO HUMOUR IN THEIR WRITTEN WORDS
RELIGIOUS FOLLOWERS ARE NOT HUMOROUS
THEY CANNOT LAUGH AT THEMSELVES
THE FEAR THEY ALL FEAR IS BEING LAUGHED AT
BEING RIDICULED FOR THEIR FAITHFUL BELIEFS
IF THEY CANNOT EXCEPT
HUMOROUS COMMENTS OR CRITICISM
THEN THEY DESERVE NO APOLOGY
NOTHING NOTHING AT ALL

446

ONE HAS GOT TO BECOME A FLY SPOTTER
BEFORE ONE CAN BECOME A FLY SWATTER
SO SPOT IT
BEFORE YOU SWAT IT

447

GOSSIP
LIES AND TRUTH
FAKE AND REALITY
IF NOT DEFINED
IS JUST GOSSIP
IN THE MURKY WORLD OF GOSSIP
WHERE ALL PLAGIARISTS PLAGUE
THEIR WHERES & WHYS FOR THEIR MASTERS

KINGS AND GOVERNMENTS
POPES AND CORPORATIONS
THE PEOPLE MUST BE KEPT FED
BY THE WILLS OF THEIR MASTERS INTENTIONS

448

IF BEING FUSSY
IS BEING CONCERNED WITH EMPATHY
THEN I HOLD MY HANDS UP GUILTY
I AM FUCKING FUSSY

449

CONTEMPLATE LIFE
LIVING IN A SERIES OF ROOMS
ROOMS THAT INTER CONNECT INTERCHANGE INTERACT
INTERNATIONAL MULTI FLOORED AND DETACHED
ROOMS THAT ARE DULL
BRIGHT AIRY OR THATCHED
ONE BECOMING THE INMATES
THAT THE ROOM ATTRACTS

450

VEILS AND CAPES
MASKS AND SHROUDS
TOO MANY TWO FACES
TO MASTER AND UNDERSTAND
THE STRAIGHT JACKET EMOTIONS
FRUSTRATIONS SCREAMS OUT LOUD
DEAF TO ALL NEW COMERS
TO THEIR ALPHABETIC LAND
LOST INTERPRETATIONS
TRANSLATIONS COMPLEX

BLIND TO EMOTIONS
DEAF TO COMPREHEND
INVISIBLE REALITY
FAKE WORLD EXISTS
CATCH A GLIMPSE CATCH A BUBBLE
CATCH A RAINBOWS END
IT'S ALL As & Cs
Os & 1s even Ys & Zs
EVERY WINDOW EVERY PORT HOLE
OPPORTUNITIES TO SEIZE
THE MOMENT THE RECOGNITION
THE LOVE BETWEEN ALL OF US
IF A is FOR ALPHA
Z is FOR ZUS

451

I LOOK AT MY SELFI
I SEE NO DIFFERENCE
UNTIL I CONVERSE
AND THEY SAY YOUR VEGAN
THEY'RE EITHER IN YOUR FACE
OR THEY LOOK AWAY
THERES NO MIDDLE ISLE
THEY'RE EITHER VILE
OR IN DENIAL
MEAT AIN'T SWEET
IT'S FULL OF SHIT
LIKE CARCINOGENIC
YOUR BETTER OFF ON LETTUCE
YOU ARE WHAT YOU EAT
YOU DON'T WANT BULL IT'S BULLSHIT
YOU NEED TO EAT PLANTS THAT GROW BRO
WE CAN ALL EAT AND REAP AS WE SOW
EVERYTHING YOU EAT DRINK WEAR AND SMOKE GROWS

THE LIVESTOCK IS NOT HEALTHY
LET THEM DIE THEY'RE NOT WELL
THEY ARE PUMPED FULL OF ANTIBIOTICS
AND STEROIDS JUST LIKE SOME OF YOU
EATING HOT DOGS AND MILK SMOOTHIES
SMILE TAKE A SELFI SAY MOO WHO

452

I'VE STARTED RAPPING ALREADY
AND IT'S NOT EVEN CHRISTMAS
WITH FOOD BANKS THEY'RE HEAVING
THAT'S WHERE I FIND MY SISTERS
IT'S FOOD ON THE TABLE
THAT WE ALL NEED TO EAT
AND THAT INCLUDES EVERYONE
WE DON'T HAVE TO COMPETE
I REPEAT
WHERE IS THE WISDOM
AND THE KNOWLEDGE IN THIS
THAT TO EAT YOU MUST FIRST
COMPLY & COMPETE
THE OUTCOME OF ALL OF THIS
IS IRRELEVANT AND INCOMPLETE
BECAUSE THIS SYSTEM ENSURES
ONLY THE FEW AT THE TOP TABLE EAT

453

ONE DOES NOT NEED
TO LOOK FOR LOVE
ONE JUST NEEDS TO RECOGNISE IT
UP GARDEN PATHS TO EDENS
FAKE SHOWS REALITY WORLDS
WHERE ANYTHING GOES
WHERE NOTHING GROWS
EXCEPT HOLES IN EGOS
AND THERE YOU GO
TO RECOGNISE LOVE
ONE WILL JUST KNOW

454

ARE WE OR ARE WE NOT ABLE
ALL OF US HERE ARE WE NOT ABLE
TO DIGEST THE DATA DISCUSS AND DEBATE ALL
THE DECISIONS THEY MAKE TO KEEP US ALL DISABLE
AWAY FROM THE DISCUSSION TABLE
WHERE THEY TAKE ALL THE PROBABLES
AND SELL US THE IMPOSSIBLES
MAKING LISTS OF THE COMPARABLE
AND ALL WHO COMPLY AND ARE ABLE
TO ENFORCE THE FEASIBLE ADMIRABLE
AUSTERITY FRAUD

455

RACE AND FAITH DISCRIMINATE
IT SEPARATES AND DIVIDES
WEALTH DIVIDES THE POOR
CULTURAL DIVIDES AND MUCH MORE
LANGUAGE AND DIALECTS
COLOUR AND POLITICS
BRITAIN OR BRITISH
WE SPEAK ENGLISH
IN THE BRITISH ISLES OF IRONY
WE EMBRACE IMMIGRATION
WITH ALL THE COLOURS IT ENTAILS

456

I AM AN OLD STURDY OAK
STRONG TO THE CORE
BUT YEW ARE AS SUPPLE AS A HAZEL
WITH A HEART OF OAK
HOLDING UP THE SKY IN YOUR
SPLENDID EVERGREEN COAT

457

CAPITALISM WORKS FOR
EVERY MAN FOR HIMSELF
SOCIALISM WORKS FOR
EVERY MAN WOMAN AND CHILD
ONE CAN STILL BE A SELFISH
COMPETITIVE EGOCENTRIC
WORKING HARD TO MAKE
LOTS & LOTS OF MONEY
IN A SOCIALIST WORLD

458

POOR PEOPLE WORK
MAKE AND CREATE
THE PRIVILEGED CLASS JUST MANAGE
TO DIRECT AND DICTATE

459

OH THE TORMENT THE STRAIN OF FAME
THE ADULATION AND COMPENSATIONAL GAIN
IT DROVE THEM TO EAT
IT DROVE THEM TO DRINK
IT DROVE THEM THROUGH DRUGS
AND OVER THE BRINK
AND AS LONG AS THEY ARE STILL ABLE TO THINK
BEFORE SIGNING THEIR NEW CONTRACT
IN FRONT OF THEM IN INK

460

PUBLIC SCHOOLS
MUST BE HELD ACCOUNTABLE
FOR THE INSTITUTIONALISED EDUCATION
OF THE PRIVILEGED CLASS
SHROUDING THEIR INTERBRED
DYSFUNCTIONAL INABILITIES
BY SPEAKING THE QUEENS ENGLISH
WEARING A SAVILE ROW SUIT
AND UPPING THEIR VOLUME
WHEN NEEDED TO BE HEARD
AND USING SLANDEROUS INSULTS AND
ACCUSATIONS IS THE ACCEPTABLE LANGUAGE
OF THESE IGNORANT NAIVE
SPOILT LITTLE SCHOOL BOYS WHERE
ARGUMENTS AND COMPETITIVE NAME CALLING
SEEMS TO BE THE PUBLIC SCHOOLS
ASPIRING DIPLOMA
TO BECOME DIPLOMATS

461

FICKLE FASHION FEATURES FRONT PAGE
FISCAL FINANCE FURTHERS FUTURES AGE
FAIR BUT NOT FAR FROM FALLING FLAT
FOREVER FEEL THE FABRIC OF THE FEISTY
FASHIONABLE FINANCIAL FRAUD

462

SOCIAL CLEANSING
IS UNFOLDING
SPLIT AND DIVIDE
KEEP THEM CRAWLING
SOCIAL CLEANSING
SHALL TALLY IT'S TOLL
AS THE WORST GOVERNMENT
OF IT'S PEOPLE MAY
THE TRUTH BE TOLD

463

500 BALLOONS IN A ROOM
NO ONE HEARD A PIN DROP

464

ONE DOES NOT SUBMIT TO RELIGION
REPETITIVE PRAYERS
REPETITIVE MANTRAS
REPETITIVE SCRIPTURES
REPETITIVE HAIL MARY'S
REPETITIVE BEAD COUNTING
REPETITIVE HEAD BANGING
ONE DOES NOT SUBSCRIBE TO
MASS SUBMISSIVE HYSTERICAL FAITH
RESULTING IN AN APATHY OF BLIND BELIEF

465

HOW DID WE GET HERE
HOWEVER WE GOT HERE
WATER AIR EARTH & FIRE
ALL WE ALIENS NEED AND DESIRE
PEACE FOOD LOVE & DREAMS
ARE PRESENTED AS CARROTS
AND RED HERRINGS IT SEEMS
WE ONLY CAME HERE
TO REPLENISH AND LEAVE
LIFE ON EARTH TAKES TIME
ONE BELIEVES

466

SOCIETIES THAT BELIEVE IN FAIRY TALES
JUST KEEP PEOPLES AND THEIR EGOS
OVER FED IN STUPIDITY WITH MUTUAL
ILLUSIONS FROM PRIESTS MULLERS AND
RABBIS ENCOURAGING THEIR CONGREGATIONS
TO THEIR SERMONS AND VIRTUES
THERE'S A HOLE IN THE ROOF

467

I WAS BROUGHT UP IN A VILLAGE WITH FRIENDS
WHEN I WOKE UP I KNEW THIS WAS NOT MY END
SO I READ AND LEARNT I WAS IN FAIRYLAND
WITH EVERYBODY BELIEVING IN SUPERMAN
SO I WENT TO TOWN AND READ THE SCORE
THERE WERE ATHEISTS THERE
THEY DON'T BELIEVE ANYMORE
AND VEGANS WHO ONLY EAT
WHAT THEY DON'T WANT TO BE
A COW A FISH A BABY LAMB MAYBE
THERE WAS SO MUCH TO READ
I WENT TO THE CITY
I LEARNT ABOUT ALL THE DRUGS
THE LEGAL BAD ILLEGAL GOOD & PRETTY
SUPPRESSED BY RELIGIONS
FALSE FED BY TECHNICIANS
DECEIVED BY POLITICIANS
THERE'S ONLY ONE PLACE LEFT SPACE
OH NO THAT'S FULL OF OUR WASTE

468

ONLY A MAN WHO HAS
CONQUERED ALL OPPOSITION
PROCLAIMS HIMSELF KING
THERE IS NO OTHER AUTHORITY
ON EARTH THUS
ALL KINGDOMS WERE WON
MAINLY BY THE BLADE & GUN
NOW ALL KINGDOMS
SHOULD BE CHALLENGED
ON THEIR AUTONOMY
BY SOMEBODY OR SOMEONE

469

SPARE PRINCE HARRY
THE GOSSIP AND THE JOKES
HIS BEST MAN HIS BRO
THE HEIR APPARENT
A JOLLY GOOD BLOKE
FOR ACCEPTING THE ACTRESS
TO THE FIRM OF THE QUEEN
MOST PROBABLY WILL BE
H R H PRINCESS MEGHAN
BY THE TIME OF HIGH TEA

470

IS IT JUST ME
WHEN I THINK OF A ROYAL WEDDING
I THINK OF THE HOMELESS
WHEN I THINK OF WHAT THEY ARE EATING
I THINK OF WHAT THE HOMELESS DON'T
WHEN I THINK OF ALL THEIR WASTE
I THINK OF FOOD BANKS
WHEN I SEE HAUTE COUTURE
I THINK OF SPORTS DIRECT AND
BRITISH HOME STORES OWNERS
WHEN I HEAR THEM SINGING WITH CHOIRS
I FEAR THE HOMELESS ARE SICK AND CRYING
WHEN THEY ALL COME OUT LAUGHING
I FEAR IT'S TOO LATE
FOR SOME ARE DEAD
AND OTHERS ARE DYING

471

CASH FOR CHAOS
THE TRUTH DOES NOT LIE
LIKE IT USED TO ANYMORE
WITH FAKE IN TRUTHS WAKE
AMERICAS FOREIGN POLICY
DESTRUCT TO CONSTRUCT

472

THE JEW IN ME ASKS YOU THE JEW
TO DRAW A MAP OF THE MIDDLE EAST TO YOU
THE ZIONIST IN ME KNOWS PALESTINE ISRAEL IS TRUE
BUT THERE IS NO PALESTINE ON THE MAP YOU DREW

473

BLUEBELLS AND SEA SHELLS
RED RIBBONS BLOW STREAMS TO RIVERS FLOW
MARBLE PILLARS AND SATIN PILLOWS
MARBLES PLAYED UNDER FIGS AND ROSE
SCULPTURES CHISELED WITH HAMMER BLOWS
THE SEEDS OF CREATION THAT LEADS ONE TO KNOW
MAN STATUE IN THE LIKENESS OF ME
LETS BRING IT UP TO DATE SMILE TAKE A SELFI

474

HOLD THE FRONT PAGE SCOOP
HOW TO GET RID OF ONES' FAMILY
IN ONE FOWL SWOOP
TELL THE TRUTH

475

IT IS NOW TIME TO CHOOSE
TO LEAVE ALL RELIGIOUS GANGS
WHO ARE ALL CULPABLE TO
THE RAPIST THE PAEDOPHILE
AND THE EXTORTIONISTS
AND BEHAVE DECENTLY AND
HONESTLY FOR ONCE
AND STOP REGISTERING YOUR
GANGS AS CHARITIES
PUTTING THE FEAR OF GOD
INTO ALL THEIR CONGREGATIONS
TO BE CHARITABLE AND TO
PAY FOR THEIR SINS
AFTER PRAYERS
AND BEFORE ONE LEAVES

476

GENDER OFFENDER
DENIES GENDER
GENDER BENDERS ARE
GENDER MENDERS

477

PARDON ME
PRESIDENT DONALD TRUMP
SIGNED
PRESIDENT DONALD TRUMP

478

I TAUGHT MY TWO BOYS
EVERYTHING I KNEW
HOW TO BLOW SMOKE RINGS
THROUGH MY MOUTH AND MY NOSE
THAT WAS THE WORST THING I EVER DID
BUT I TELL YOU NOW I NEVER HIT MY KIDS
SOCIAL MANNERS & POLITENESS CAME TOP OF THE LIST
I NEVER TAUGHT THEM TO DECEIVE DENY OR GET PISSED
STILL ONE CAN'T GET A CUCKOO TO BUILD A NEST
AND ONE GETS CARRIED AWAY BY OTHERS WHO KNOW BEST
AND AS ONE BECOMES THE COMPANY THEY KEEP
PRUDENCE ASKS
IS ONE BECOMING A SHEEP

479

ONE MAY TEACH
AND EDUCATE
BUT ONE CANNOT TEACH
COMPREHENSION MATE

480

GRIEF IS JUST LOVE
WITH NO WHERE TO GO

481

THE LAUGHTER
THE HYSTERICAL LAUGHTER
THE SCREAMS THE CRIES
THOSE EERIE LONG CRIES
AS THE KNIVES COME OUT
EVERYONE SHOUTS
AS GUNS ARE PULLED OUT
BULLETS FLY ABOUT
AS THE CRIES AND SCREAMS
MELD AS ONE IT SEEMS
LIFE FADES TO DEATH IT LEAVES
SILENCE IN THEIR WAKE
IS THERE BREATH ONE BREATHES
IN THE SILENCE
IT'S THE BREATH OF LIFE ONE BREATHES IN
AND THEN THE LAUGHTER

482

BEAUTY IS IN THE EYES OF THE BEHOLDER
AS IS HATE & RELIGION
SO WHAT OF PEACE & LOVE

483

THE MEEK WHO SHOULD INHERIT THE WORLD
ARE CONTINUOUSLY PICKED ON BY BULLY BOY BAILIFFS
AT THE LEGAL WHIMS OF CERTAIN COUNCILS AND
PARTICULAR POLITICAL PARTIES
THE POOR THE LONELY THE WEEK THE ELDERLY
THE DISABLED THE MENTALLY CHALLENGED
THE DEAF DUMB AND BLIND
AND ALL THE PEOPLE WITH DISEASE
YOU ARE ALL SOLD A BETTER CLASS VOTE
AS YOU'LL ALL PAY THROUGH THE NOSE
MAY IT STICK IN YOUR THROAT

484

MAN EXISTS LIKE A PIN PRICK
ON EARTHS BALLOON SURFACE

485

THE BLISS OF IGNORANCE
GOVERNS OUR SHORES
AS MAY THE BLISS MACHINE POURS
MORE OIL ON TROUBLED WATERS
PHILIP MAY MAKES MORE MONEY FROM
MEDICAL MARIJUANA GROWN HERE & SOLD ABROAD
TERESA MAYS GOVERNMENT MAKES TAXES ON THIS
AND WITH ELECTIONS COMING UP NEEDS VOTES AND INSISTS
LEGALISING MEDICAL MARIJUANA HAS NOTHING TO DO WITH PHIL
TAXES PROFITS OR VOTES IT IS ALL IN THE BILL

486

I HAVE BEEN A FEMINIST
ALL MY ADULT LIFE
I FELL IN LOVE WITH A GIRL
WHO WAS MORE FEMINIST THAN ME
WHY HAS NO QUEEN NOR
FEMALE PRIME MINISTER
EVER TAKEN THE STAND FOR
EQUAL GENDER & FEMINISM
IT HAS BEEN LEFT IN THE LONG GRASS
FOR FAR TOO LONG AND NOW
WOMEN HAVE GOT UP OFF THEIR KNEES
AND STOOD UP TO THE STATUS QUO
THAT DISCRIMINATES BETWEEN WE THE SEXES
THE BATTLE OF THE SEXES FEMALE & MALE HAS BEGUN
I MARK MINE DEMOCRATICALLY FEMINIST

487

ONE NEVER KNOWS WHAT IS AROUND THE BEND
AS ONE PREPARES TO ASCEND OR DESCEND
FOR IT ALL REALLY DOES DEPEND
UPON ALL THINGS BEING RELEVANT IN THE END

488

ON BEHALF OF ALL PARENTS & TEACHERS WORLDWIDE
OUTSIDE TOILET WC BATHROOM WASHROOM
COME OUT WITH YOUR HANDS WASHED
SCRIPTED FOR ALL HYGIENE PURPOSES

489

WHAT PRICE IS ONE PREPARED TO PAY
AT THE END OF EACH DAY
THE PRICE OF SLEEP
DOES IT COME CHEAP
THE WORK YOU DO
IS IT NOT YOU
ONE HIDES IN FEAR
UNDER LAUGHTER AND DEBT
AFRAID TO LET GO
AND LET YOU COME OUT
THE LIFE ONE DESERVES
FREE AND SELFLESS
THE PRICE OF PEACE
PRICELESS

490

WHAT'S YOUR PROBLEM
WHATEVER IT IS
LOOK IN THE MIRROR
AND LISTEN TO THIS
PERSONS PROBLEMS
THEIR TALES OF WOE
YOU SHOULD HAVE
YOU SHOULDN'T HAVE
YOU MUST NEVER
JUST SAY NO
THE WORDS THE DOUBT
THE REASONS THE WIT
THE WISDOM IS IN THE TRUTH
YOU TWIT

491

COPULATION FORNICATION
PROCREATION SEXUALISATION
IN THE SEA AIR AND ON LAND
SEX IS EVERYWHERE
ONE COULD SAY JOLLY GOOD LUCK
ON THE OTHER HAND
WE'RE ALL FUCKED
AND MOST PROBABLY EATEN

492

NOTHING SEEMS TO MATTER
WITH EYES CLOSED
LIKE A CAMERA SHUTTER
MEMORIES AND VISIONS
WHATEVER ONES' SEEN
SCREENING AND SCROLLING
FLOOD LIT SCENES
A GARDEN A BUILDING
A TURN PIKE ROAD
A VIEW FROM A TRAVELING TRAIN
A FERRIS WHEEL OR A FLYING PLANE
THEY'RE FROM YOUR CHILDHOOD
A YEAR AGO OR JUST LAST WEEK
MEMORIES ARE FOREVER ONES' TO KEEP

493

THE FUTURE DESERVES THE TRUTH
FAKE FALSE AND FABRICATED
IN THE FAIRYLAND FILES OF FICTITIOUS
RELIGIOUS CULTURAL INDOCTRINATIONS
KINGS & QUEENS OBLIGED TO BELIEVE
PRIME MINISTERS & CABINET MEMBERS
POMPOUSLY PRETEND TO BELIEVE
IN THE SUBORDINATIONS OF THEIR SUBJECTS
MAY THE FUTURE RESERVE THE TRUTH AS MAN
BLUNDERS BLINDLY BEYOND THE BOUNDARIES OF BIGOTRY
BOLT ONESELF DOWN STRAP ONESELF IN
THE NEXT CHAPTER OF MAN IS ABOUT TO BEGIN

494

MORALS I STARTED TO SAY
MORALS ARE YES
THEY'RE ON THE HIGH STREET
OPPOSITE THE ALCOHOL ARMS
NO MORALS MORALITY
AH YOU'VE GOT ME THERE
ISN'T THAT THE CONTINUE
TRUMP REALITY SHOW
NO I MEAN PRINCIPLES
OH THATS THE 5 STAR HOTEL
ON THE MAIN INTERSECTION ROUNDABOUT

495

ACCEPT GOD EXISTS
AND ONE ACCEPTS ALL THE BAGGAGE
LIES AND SHIT THAT GO ALONG WITH IT
ACCEPT CARNIVOROUS FOOD
AND ONE ACCEPTS THE TORTURED RAPE REARING
OF ANIMALS FEARFUL PAIN IN ONES DIET
ACCEPT LEGAL CLASS A DRUGS
ALCOHOL & TOBACCO
AND ONE ACCEPTS ONE IS
PAYING IN TAX TO KILL ONESELF

496

RED POPPIES AND WHITE POPPIES GROW TO PLEASE
RED POPPIES AND WHITE POPPIES STAND FOR WAR AND PEACE

497

LIFE IS NOT A TEST
A GAME A PLAY AN ACT
THERE'S NO DRESS REHEARSAL LIFE'S REAL
THERE'S NO PRETENSE IN FACT
LIFE ENDS LIKE A LEAF
FALLING TREE WITH DEAD ROOTS
LIVE LIFE NOW WITH LOVE
FILL YOUR BOOTS

498

PLUG YOURSELF INTO THE NIGHT
STREAM AND DREAM
AS YOU SLEEP YOU MIGHT
SOLVE AN ALGORITHM RIDDLE
WHILST REJUVENATING TO ENERGISE
YOURSELF TO HAVE A PIDDLE

499

BEING THE ONE AND ONLY
ELEPHANT IN THE ROOM
ONE SHOULD BE ALLOWED TO
BLOW ITS OWN TRUMPET VERY LOUD
IN CASE ONE SHOULD FORGET TOO SOON
WE ARE ALL THE ELEPHANTS IN THE ROOM

500

THEIR TIMELESS MASS EXISTENCE
RELIES ON MANS ATOMIC AGE
BOUND BY ALL THE ELEMENTS
WE SHARE WITH THESE BEAUTIFUL CREATURES
MAN HAS LEARNT NOTHING FROM ELEPHANTS
SO LET THEIR TRUMPETING
BE HEARD FOREVER
AND MAY THE HUMANS LISTEN
TO THE ELEPHANTS IN THE ROOM
AS THEY PACKED THEIR TRUNKS
AND SAID GOODBYE
TO THE HUMAN CIRCUS
WITH A TRUMPITY TRUMP